"Is the human brain created in the image of God, including the parts impacted by mental illness? Jeff Hood argues for a theology that takes seriously God's intimate knowledge of mental illness, inviting us to see God suffering with us and saving us. At times disturbing and ultimately hopeful, this book is a welcomed addition to the conversation of the intersection of mental health and Christianity. Hood testifies to the expansive reach of God's love, even into the most diseased and disordered parts of the brain."

—**Sarah Griffith Lund**, Author of *Blessed are the Crazy: Breaking the Silence About Mental Illness, Family and Church*

"The Reverend Dr. Jeff Hood has penned yet another uncomfortable book. For some, *The Psychosis of God* will prove unnerving because of the topic; for others, because of the writing itself, which borders on the manic; and for those of us who are non-theists, because of the unrelentingly theological approach. And yet, this is a worthwhile read, perhaps even a necessary one. Right and wrong, beauty and ugliness, angels and demons —all dualities are mere appearances, conceptual constructs arising, enduring briefly, and subsiding in the empty luminosity of the unborn mind. Dr. Hood invites us to visit this luminous perfection, this emptiness where all is possible, the good and the bad."

—**Tashi Nyima**, New Jonang Buddhist Community

"While most of Christianity is stuck in an ableist theology of Platonic ideals, Rev. Hood seeks to provide liberation: liberation from thinking that our minds and bodies must be normalized, by showing us that even God has struggled. This book shows why it is vital to have theologies from marginalized and non-normative voices. May we all be challenged to see God's image in ourselves."

—**Ember Kelley**, Transgender Faith Activist

"In his newest book, Dr. Jeff Hood continues fulfilling his call to queer prophetic troublemaking. In the true spirit of liberation theology, Dr. Hood reminds us that God is with us, whether we're perceived to be perfect or defective. God joins us in our psychosis because God is one of us."

—**Mike Wright-Chapman**, Funeral Director

"Dr. Jeff Hood has done it again. He has both challenged and inspired while offering imagery that gives us a rare glimpse of the face of God. This book, as Hood describes it, is an exploration. While I agree that it is an exploration of God in the marginalization of the mentally ill, I also believe it is an exploration of the reader's own soul. This text beckons us within, demands that we question our preconceived notions of the Divine, and takes us on a journey to discover the face of God in ways we have not; namely in those who experience mental illness. It is a telling and intimate look into a life and experience many have never seen. Hood bears his own vulnerability and should be applauded for kicking down the door of stigma. There is indeed a balm in Gilead...and for many, it will be found in this book."

—**Ray Jordan**, United Church of Christ Pastor

"At once a broken laughing lament and a complex midrash for creation, *The Psychosis of God* embraces all the thrills and horrors of our craziness. Hood continues to press us into an every-expanding gallery of inclusive images of God and ourselves."

—**Imam La Trina Jackson**, Islamic Thinker and Activist

"A raw and powerful account of suffering that passionately dismantles a construction of a rational God inherited from Judeo-Christian tradition."

—**Terry Barrett**, Professor Emeritus, The Ohio State University

"I am most aware of my own spiritual growth in the moments when I realize my personal relationship with God, and that of my neighbor, is far more personal than I could have ever imagined. Rev. Jeff Hood's work to unveil the psychosis of God both illuminated another way in which God walks with us stride for stride, and reflects Rev. Hood's dedication to the holy mission of creating space for heaven on earth."

—**Joe Swanson**, American Civil Liberties Union

"Jeff Hood dares us to affirm the radical implications of our belief in both the Imago Dei and the Incarnation. If people with mental disorders are made in God's likeness, then what, exactly, is the divine image being reflected? If God in Christ identifies with humanity, does God identify with us all the way down?"

—**Matt Johnson**, Cooperative Baptist Fellowship Pastor

"This book is of work of courage and honesty and it is an important contribution to the task of re-membering the human family. The stigma, shame, and isolation directed towards so many has also eaten away at our capacity to come nearer to the incomprehensible person of God."

—**Lucas Johnson**, International Pastor and Thinker

"Dr. Jeff Hood is pushing us to new enlightenment. He detangles what we tangle, and challenges us to be better lovers of one another."

—**Celeste Holbrook**, Sex Therapist

"Jeff Hood always finds a way to make the deeply prophetic meet the deeply personal. In *The Psychosis of God*, his words offer comfort, challenge, and most of all, hope. He calls us to care and to believe that we are all the created, beloved ones of God."

—**Leah Grundset Davis**, Communications Specialist, Alliance of Baptists

"The way Jeff Hood uses words will push you. It may anger you. However, if you can get past your anger and discomfort and allow the prophetic beauty of his words to resonate in your soul, you will be changed. Let Jeff take you beyond language to the mind of God."

—**Andrew Robinson**, Recovering Pastor and Activist

"As the Father of a schizophrenic adult son, I've had many conversations with Jeff Hood on mental illness, and I have never left a conversation with him in which I didn't learn something or question something. The same is true with this book. There are no solutions here. There are lots of questions. Questions that made me think."

—**Mike Renquist**, President/Owner, OnSite Training and Consultation

"'God is sick.' So begins Jeff Hood's challenging *The Psychosis of God*. It is a much-needed look at God through the lens of mental illness—both Jeff's and God's. Grounded in liberation theologies, which explore God through the lens of oppression and marginalization, and in queer theology, which maintains that God is found in those who are strange or non-normative, it will be especially helpful for those who are mentally ill. It will also be welcome for those who cherish hope-providing inventiveness in theology. This is an intensely personal volume which no one but Jeff could have written—desperate, off-the-chain, encouraging, and brave. A masterpiece."

—**Ellin Jimmerson**, Radical Baptist Prophet

"For anyone who is tired of normative theology, which continues to rehash propositional statements from people in power, this book by Jeff Hood will be an eye-opener. It will challenge you and broaden the way you think about God and faith. At times it will feel like heresy. But at times you will experience liberation. Hood continues to take a risk in the way he thinks about God in order to free the prophetic imagination."

—**Danny Cortez**, Southern Baptist Exile

"I have come to depend on Jeff Hood to help me think about matters of theology in a fresh, imaginative, and insightful way. I am exceedingly grateful for his passion."

—**Lee Ann Bryce**, Queer United Church of Christ Pastor

"*The Psychosis of God* invites us all into the holy discomfort of an imperfectly perfect God through the lens of mental illness. Dr. Hood so vulnerably and candidly gives sight to how ill-equipped the church universal is in getting over its own stigmatization of mental illness. Hood shares with us the good news that no mental instability of any kind can ever separate us from our innate divinity, we always remain God's holy creation, simultaneously imperfect and perfect. This is what it means to be human."

—**Kyndra Frazier**, Queer Licensed Social Worker

"Once again, Jeff explores a new way of exploring the depths of the Divine. What I enjoy the most about reading Jeff's work is how he pushes boundaries and challenges me to examine my faith in refreshing ways. Because of this book, I'm thinking and rethinking the who, what, when, where, how, and why of God once again."

—**Kyle Tubbs**, Peace of Christ Church

"Jeff has the unique ability to place God across the kitchen table from us through his writing, which creates the intimacy necessary to discuss such topics. Nothing is off limits while all is still held sacred. I admire his ability to witness to mental illness with honesty, humor and compassion."

—**Bojangles Blanchard**, Queer Baptist Prophet

"My father, also a pastor, always said that those we labeled 'crazy' among us were actually the closest to God. Jeff Hood breaks down that assertion in The Psychosis of God and takes it one step further, claiming God's self is mentally ill. In a country where over a quarter of the population has a diagnosable mental disorder in any given year, Hood's provocative book will challenge you to wrestle with the reality of mental illness and the Imago Dei, providing a path of liberation for us all."

—**Kristin Stoneking**, Executive Director, Fellowship of Reconciliation

THE PSYCHOSIS OF GOD

THE PSYCHOSIS OF GOD

An Exploration of Mental Illness

Jeff Hood

Foreword by Emily Jean Hood

WIPF & STOCK · Eugene, Oregon

Wipf & Stock
An Imprint of Wipf and Stock Publishers
199 W. 8th Ave., Suite 3
Eugene, OR 97401

www.wipfandstock.com

PAPERBACK ISBN: 978-1-4982-9898-8
HARDCOVER ISBN: 978-1-4982-9900-8
EBOOK ISBN: 978-1-4982-9899-5

Manufactured in the U.S.A.   SEPTEMBER 7, 2016

For the Crazy

Contents

Foreword

WHEN I MET JEFF HOOD, I knew mental illness was part of the package. However, I had no idea what that meant. Over the past five years, I've gained tremendous insight, though I also understand that the human mind is something that can never be fully known. Kind of like God. The mind knows in part and the mind is known in part. That means that there is much we do not know about ourselves, and there is much we do not know about God. What do we do with the mystery of it all?

In the summer of 2011, I was living in rural central Texas working as an artist. There weren't many people around my age, so online dating seemed like a good option. I knew it would open my world to folks I might not cross paths with otherwise. I've always loved adventure, and it seemed like a rather adventurous thing to do. Two years into the endeavor, I found myself disillusioned with the process and the people I was (or wasn't) meeting. I met a few diamonds, but no one that fit the bill for a life companion. I lamented to my friend Sarah, sad that I felt so out of place in life. I was moving away from my family in a theological sense, and I wanted to find someone who understood the world the way that I did. The next morning, I received a message from a guy named Jeff. My first thought was, wow—this guy doesn't look like all the other guys (he was wearing really cool glasses). There was also something familiar about his face. It sounds cliché, but I felt like I already knew him. Over the course of the next few days, as I traveled and camped in the Sangre de Cristo Mountains of Norther

New Mexico, Jeff and I shared long phone conversations. Early on he told me that he had a mental illness. It was shocking, but I appreciated his transparency. Our relationship moved rather quickly from there. We met in person over the next few weeks and continued our relationship long distance. We decided to get married, so two months after we met we married.

Since then, life has been a blur. We moved to Tupelo, Mississippi so that Jeff could pursue graduate studies at the University of Mississippi. I painted, taught art lessons and worked at Starbucks. I was doing community theater when I found out I was pregnant with twins. In the meantime, I was offered a full scholarship and teaching fellowship to the doctoral program in art education at the University of North Texas. That spring brought with it the deepest depression I have ever witnessed in another human being. Jeff constantly talked about suicide. He struggled to get out of bed in the mornings. We prayed together at night, and he would always say, "God, we pray to you because we don't know what else to do." Jeffrey and Phillip were born at the end of May. Phillip had some breathing issues and spent a week in NICU. I thought it was the end of the world. Postpartum depression was in full force. I was sleep deprived. A hormonal wreck. I felt doomed. We hadn't been married a year and we were dealing with the crazy web we had woven.

After a few visits with different psychiatrists, Jeff received a new diagnosis and started on new medicine. Things got worse before they got better, but eventually we found a point of relative stability. We moved to Texas when the babies were three months old and I started PhD work. I loved it. It was my bliss.

After lunch at the park with the babies and my friend Channelle, I realized I had a significant sunburn. When you are pregnant you are more susceptible to sunburn. My suspicions were confirmed by a home pregnancy test. I was happy, though I wondered what this would mean for my studies. We kept going.

Quinley was born in a therapy pool in our living room in early December. Jeff was the best birth partner. He stayed in the water with me at the end and applied counter pressure to my back for an hour or more. He is loyal and determined—a theme that often resounds in the vessel of our marriage. I again struggled with postpartum depression. I remember that Jeff and I were arguing, yelling at each other one morning. I left to go take a shower. Sobbing as the water splashed down on my face I knew our marriage was falling apart. I thought it was over . . . based on one fight. My ability to reason logically was completely shot.

After the birth, Jeff lost his mind. On multiple occasions, Jeff described seeing things that were not there. There was no way to make it stop. Jeff kept swinging back and forth between mania and depression with a touch of paranoia and hallucination thrown in. I didn't know what to do. I just prayed. The days and nights got worse before they got better. Eventually, Jeff pulled out of it. In the midst of the chaos, I always pray for Jeff to pull out of it.

On and off, we talked about having another baby. An even number of kids seemed like a good idea, and since the first three were so close in age, we went for it. A couple of weeks in, I felt horrible and started having flashbacks to my first pregnancy. I knew I was pregnant with multiples—I feared it might be triplets! The doctor confirmed my suspicions, and once again we were having twins. It was a difficult time. For me, twin pregnancy was physically and emotionally draining, and even still, there were three little people who needed constant support. I carried the babies to full term. I felt so many things that I can't begin to describe. I thought I was going to die. But amid the struggle, I was excited to meet the babies. This time around, I realized that something about impending childbirth triggered Jeff's depression. So, all of these obstacles seemed to come at once. When the babies finally arrived, we ended up with one vaginal birth and one emergency C-section. We were grateful for the health and safety of our babies, but I was spent emotionally and physically. Despite these obstacles, we made it through.

I will never forget the day that my Mom, my Aunt, and I stood in my grandfather's kitchen discussing the arrival of the second set of twins. They looked me straight in the eye, and with deep concern and disbelief said, "How will you ever take care of five little children!?" At the time I was really hurt by their lack of hope for the situation. I told them, "I don't' know! I've never taken care

of five kids before! I do know we won't all just lay down and die."
I guess that was my way of sticking up for myself. What I should
have said was, it hurts my feeling that you said that. What I need
now is love, support, and encouragement. I don't have room for
negativity and fear.

I relay that story to illustrate something very special about
my relationship with Jeff Hood. Despite the challenges that we
have faced over these five years. Despite a constant juggling of
mental stability for both of us. Despite the demands of exponen-
tial family growth. We are committed to hope. We are committed
to asking questions. And we are committed to creating a world
that is not dominated by fear and rules. We believe that the image
of God makes it thus, and if we are to be faithful, we must move
forward, side by side, notwithstanding the expectations and fears
of our world.

This creative way of living is complicated. It is full of un-
knowns as we forge new paths. But, it is a divine right and the
pathway of freedom. As such, I return to the idea of the God we
cannot fully know. The God in whose image we are created. There
are fundamental characteristics that belong to the Divine. Love
being the foremost. How do we imagine the love of God for the
mentally ill? How have our churches extended divine love to the
mentally ill? What does our society have to say about the mentally
ill? You can take the time to answer each of these questions, and I
think you will find incongruence and failures. The mentally ill are
marginalized. They are defective. We are afraid of mental illness.
Perhaps in this day and age, Jesus would say, "Blessed are the mentally ill, for they will experience the world in profound ways." My
academic mentor always talks about how outsiders often make the
greatest theoretical contributions to any given discipline or field
because they are able to see that particular world through a different lens. For many mentally ill people, the experience of the world
is never normative. Even with medication there are struggles with
each moment. Dealing with this kind of adversity, this instability,
causes one to struggle and fight to survive. For my husband, his
will to fight has ensured his survival and equipped him to do the

social justice work that he does. His grit, along with the lens God has given him, allows him to make theological innovations, such as this book. In many ways, his mental illness offers him creative affordances that others will never have. I know Jeff is not alone.

What if we apply our creativity to God as well? What if we allow ourselves to imagine God in an infinite number of ways? I believe it is important to do so with humility, knowing that for now, our knowing is partial. Nonetheless, God calls us to be co-creators. God is in our midst and we are made in God's image. For many that image includes mental illness, and so generating ideas about God based on psychosis allows those who are mentally ill to become an integral part of the flock. Many indigenous cultures have much more reverence for those whose minds allow them to experience the world in non-normative ways. Perhaps we can learn from their traditions. Perhaps we can reimagine God and in so doing reimagine mental illness, ultimately accepting it as a complex way of being that is fraught will challenges, and yet ushers unique knowledge into the world that would otherwise not exist.

This book is a theology of mental illness, and yet it is about all of us. This book emerges from Jeff's personal struggles. Though it is an intensely personal topic, it is simultaneously collective in nature. Mental illness touches all of us in one way or another. We must decide how we will respond to mental illness in various context within our culture. This book calls the reader to imagine how psychosis and mental illness might be part of God's divine perfection, and then asks the reader to apply their thoughts to practical engagements of theology in everyday life. May we never forget that the unknowable aspects of God are an invitation to imagine perfection more perfectly.

—Emily Jean Hood, May 2016

Preface

GOD IS SICK. LET every word of that statement sink in. Such thoughts make us cringe. Our earliest cultural engagements with God teach us the opposite. Our religious expectations inform us that a sick God is no God. We demand perfection from our God. Unfortunately, our thoughts of perfection are distorted around our own expectations of what perfection must look like. We assume that God must be without any type of defect. Our ideas of defection are rooted in the things that we are repulsed by. God has never engaged perfection and defection in such a way. God has always been found in spaces of defection. God has always been found with us. For God, defection is perfection and perfection is defection. *The Psychosis of God* is about finding God in defection.

Theologies of liberation begin in oppression and marginalization. Such theologies dare to construct a God that is intimately and intrinsically connected to the suffering of God's people. Liberation theologians are persons dedicated to the task of demanding the liberation of God through demanding the liberation of God's people. *The Psychosis of God* begins in a place of oppression and marginalization. The mentally ill are considered to be the most defective people in our society. Liberation theology is always about running to places of defection. Liberation theologians sprint to such places because we know that God is there. We know that God is most fully found in the oppressed and the marginalized. This liberation theology dares to imagine the movements of a mentally ill God through the movements of mentally ill people. Fighting for the liberation of the mentally ill is about fighting for the liberation of a mentally ill God. For the mentally ill, liberation comes from the wide recognition that in defection exists perfection. God is there.

Queer theologies dare to purport that God is located in that which is queer or strange amongst us. That which is queer has transcended boundaries of normativity. Mental illness has never been considered normative. The minds of the crazy are always outside of the boundaries of what society assumes normal minds are supposed to be. Normativity tells us to stay within the lines. We are told to hide everything that is outside the lines. The true queer refuses to be closeted. The true queer refuses to play by the rules. The true queer has always been considered mentally ill. God has never played by the rules. God has always refused to be closeted. God has never fit in. God has always been queer. God has always been mentally ill.

I didn't start out in defection. I started in perfection. Throughout my life, I just wanted to be perfect as I assumed God was perfect. The older I got, the more I realized that God is perfect in defection and so are we. *The Psychosis of God* is about liberating the queer mentally ill minds amongst us. Lasting liberation always begins and ends with the knowledge that your perfection is found in your defection. This is a very strange book. The mentally ill image of God is used to resurrect a mentally ill God. I proceed from my mentally ill mind to other mentally ill minds to ponder the mentally ill mind of God. This is not an exact science. This is an exploration. Some will argue that this book is crazy, they will be right.

—Rev. Dr. Jeff Hood, May 2016

Acknowledgements

THE PSYCHOSIS OF GOD is the result of many years worth of encounters with ignorant dumbasses. I remember the one who told me that the mentally ill were bound for hell. I remember one who told me that mental illness was fake. I remember the one who told me that reading the Bible would heal my mental illness. I remember all of them and more. The ignorant dumbasses provided all of the fuel that I ever could need to write this book. Thank you from the bottom of my heart.

God is nuts. I'm grateful that I've been able to engage the crazy side of God. If I hadn't been able to come to terms with my own mental illness, I don't know that I would have ever really met God. I know I was not alone in all of these explorations. Thank you God for being crazy as hell too. I wouldn't have been able to write this book without you.

I make it through life with the help of my doctors. Thank you from the depths of my mind.

Lithium also played a big part in the production of this book. Thank you for leveling me out.

Friends have talked me through various stages and manifestations of mental illness. Without their support, you would be reading my obituary. Thank you for holding me to the light.

My mentors are with me everywhere I go. Thank you for constantly pushing me.

To my family, it's good to be crazy with you. Thank you for riding this thing out with me.

My chickens are the best medicine I have ever had. Thank you for your love my feathered friends.

Emily. I can never say enough. Ours is a crazy love. I can't wait to grow crazier with you.

Jeff, Phillip, Quinley, Lucas and Madeleine. Your daddy loves you more than even the craziest minds could ever imagine. I write for you. Carry these wild words to the ends of the universe and beyond. The mentally ill God will meet you there.

Introduction

"Do not be conformed to this world . . ."—Romans 12:2

"YOU'RE CREATED IN THE image of God." During my childhood, I heard it a million times. No one knew that I was mentally ill. I guess I didn't even know. I thought crazy was normal and normal was crazy. People with mental illness were treated terribly around me. I knew God's image wouldn't be used to describe anyone like me. Nevertheless, it was. When I struggled to function, I figured God was struggling too. When I was terrified, I figured God was terrified too. I figured God knew the voices. I figured God knew the anxiety. I figured God knew the rage. I figured God knew the panic attacks. When I was told that I was created in the image of God, I believed it. After many decades of evidence that might prove otherwise, I still do.

Often, I return to those dark nights. The nights when I couldn't see. The nights when my mind got worse. The nights when nothing seemed to exist. The nights when I begged for help. The nights behind the locked door. The nights with the voices. The nights. In those moments, I return to the nights where I was created and God was too.

"How could you write such a thing? You're evil. God's not sick! You are!" I come from a world where people believe that mental illness is a result of sin. These folks think that taking medicine is like feeding a demon. Needless to say, I didn't get any sort of help or relief until long after I left fundamentalism. The further away I traveled, the more I was aware that I was mentally ill. When I started sharing what was going on with those from my past, I was belittled and treated like shit. The comments were unbeliev-able. "Those are the Devil's pills! You take those and you will be doing the Devil's work." "You've left God!" "Have you considered that you're possessed?" While I struggled for clarity in other ar-eas, I knew for a fact that these folks were definitely crazier than I was. Such thoughts were reassuring. Regardless, I tried to engage some of what they said. Everyone I talked to wanted me to think about sin. I did. The more I considered that the incarnation of God extends both to God's image in which we are made and to God's presence with those who are suffering or marginalized, the more I became convinced that God is mentally ill and always has been. My mental illness wasn't a fallen reflection of God. My mental ill-ness was the reflection of God.

"You're crazy. God's not." Though the words were different, the heartbreak was the same. When I started to share my idea of God being mentally ill, my progressive friends were just as closed off as the fundamentalists. Isn't it interesting how people feel the need to project perfection on God when God's image is always perfect? "Stop with all that crazy shit!" "Do you honestly think God takes psychotropic drugs?" Regardless of who was doing the beating, I felt ashamed of my condition. Humans can only take so much rejection. While exploring other theological paths, I put the mentally ill God in a closet of normative understanding. The world wasn't ready for me. The world wasn't ready for God. Now, I don't care. I know I'm not alone.

"Who are you?" Ms. Ruth asked me the same question every day. When I explained that I was the chaplain, I never knew what was coming next. There were only two options. Sometimes, the chaplain revelation sent her into a rage. Part of Ms. Ruth hated God and wanted to lash out at anything having to do with God. Sometimes, the chaplain revelation made her blissful. Part of Ms. Ruth loved God with all of her heart and wanted to grasp at anything having to do with God. Ms. Ruth's condition caused her to swing back and forth. I loved spending time with her because her condition reminded me so much of my own. I felt like I was looking into my future and learning to not be afraid. One day after a long talk, Ms. Ruth looked me dead in the eyes and asked me a deadly serious question, "Did God create us mentally ill?" Though I'd thought about it before, I didn't want to think about it again. If God created us mentally ill, then we were perfect in our mental illness . . . perfect in our suffering. I didn't answer Ms. Ruth right away. How could I? I was scared of what the answer could be. Finally, I raised my voice and said, "God is mentally ill." The evil hesitancies that held me back were gone. Before she left the hospital, Ms. Ruth and I had this same conversation numerous times. Though the presence was always slightly different, God never failed to meet us there.

"God, I need your help. I don't trust my brain right now." I always pray this prayer with tears in my eyes. When I manage to string these words together, I'm often at the end of my rope. Looking around, I know that I'm a danger to myself and everyone else. I just keep praying. Before I understood, I figured that God would just heal me and this would all be over. In my most desperate moments, I thought that it would be best to simply end it all. While I knew this would bring healing for me, I also knew that this would bring great sickness to those I loved. Sometimes, time grows understanding. When I realized that God was with me, I didn't need God's help. I just needed God's presence. When I didn't trust my brain, I leaned into God's brain. Then, I realized that God's brain was just as untrustworthy as mine. Together, we prayed for a future. Though I still didn't trust my brain, I trusted that somehow our brains could work together. I trusted that the mentally ill brain of God could partner with my mentally ill brain to make our way through the darkness. Together, I trusted that we could get to the switch and turn the light on. I believed that God would never leave me nor forsake. When I asked God for help, God did me one better and gave me the incarnation of God. We serve a sick God that cannot be destroyed by mental illness.

God has tried everything to get well. None of it worked. God had to keep on going. God is mentally ill. You cannot change what you are. When God learned to love God's troubled mind, God became most fully God. In God's journeys, God was able to heal and ease the mental afflictions of others because God was comfortable with God's own mental afflictions. God continues to be guided by a troubled mind. When God accepted all that God was, that troubled mind started to heal the world.

"Who is God?" The question startled the group. Spirituality groups on the psychiatric ward usually don't engage such direct questions. I decided to take a chance. "God is my savior!" "God is nothing." "God is everything!" The answers kept coming until it was time for Ms. Maggie to answer. For many months, Ms. Maggie sat in one of the rooms on the psychiatric ward. Since she refused to respond to any of the staff, everyone assumed that she couldn't talk. I did too. As I opened my mouth to try to produce meaning, Ms. Maggie spoke, "God is just as crazy as us. God lives here." Everyone was stunned. I listened to the silence. Holiness swept the room and we all knew that there was nothing left to stay. God wasn't with the patients metaphorically. God was with them in actuality. I never heard Ms. Maggie speak again. Despite my efforts to the contrary, the hospital sent her to the state mental hospital. I don't know what happened to her. I only know that her words are still with me.

People think that God is way off somewhere. People think that God has nothing in common with humans. People think that God is something other. I want people to know that God is more like them than not. God exists in the image of humans. We know that from our creation. In the midst of a psychotic breakdown, I remember Tonya crying out, "I need a God that is just as fucked up as me." A God that is not mentally ill cannot connect with those who are. Those who are mentally ill cannot intimately connect with a God who is not. By that time, I'd thought about it enough. God is mentally ill. God knows what we're going through. God is depressed. God is manic. God has unwanted thoughts. God has multiple personalities. God has it all. I've met God in all of these spaces.

Homeless, Lester prayed on the ground outside of our church. For over three weeks, I just passed by. Honestly, I was scared of what he might do. Knowing that he had serious mental issues, I didn't want to trigger him. One night, I was going to simply pass again. Then, he called out to me, "Hey preacher man! You got a God for me?" After thinking for a minute, I said, "What would you say about a mentally ill God?" For many months, we talked and dreamed. The mentally ill and God became one.

Laurie's words were disturbing. Knowing that I studied theology, she always talked about fucking God in the ass. It seemed every night the descriptions got more colorful and intense. I tried to block her out. When you rent in the same place as someone, there is only so much you can do. I wondered if she was possessed. I had no idea what was going on. In a moment of vulnerability, Laurie told me that she was "brainsick." I believed her. Not long after she told me this, Laurie went back to the bullshit. The words just kept coming. One evening, I came in and Laurie was talking suicide. Looking at me, Laurie asked, "What does your God have to say about being messed up in the head?" I replied, "God is mentally ill. God is in you right now. God created you this way." Putting down the thoughts of suicide, Laurie kept going.

I met Paul at church. I'll never forget the first night. We were living in a small place and going to a small church. Though our theology only occasionally matched their theology, we found community there. Paul gave all he had to the lights and the movements of the rhythm. While the band played, he would spit on the floor, raise his hands in the air and drop to roll around in his own spit. This was Paul's way of praising God. Folks at the church didn't like it. I've always thought it funny that religious folk like to talk about how much they love the homeless until they actually show up. Rolling in his spit, Paul got louder and louder. Some of the guys in the church moved to eject him. I stepped in. Looking one of those cats right in the eye, I declared, "If you kick him out, you are kicking out the very presence of God. Have you never read Matthew 25 asshole?" The church backed off and the service concluded. Ashamed of how he was treated, I invited Paul to stay with us. On the first night, Paul talked about killing us. On the second night, Paul described how he was going to kill us. On the third night, we felt like Paul was ready to try. Unfortunately, Paul got more violent by the hour. My wife called the police. Later, I had to testify for him to be involuntarily committed to the state mental hospital. During the proceedings, I was asked, "Do you worship the same God as Paul?" I didn't hesitate, "Of course. We've found the God that is as crazy as we are."

Before creation, God existed in the darkness. There was nothing and everything at the same time. Regardless of what was, God was really messed up. There was a loneliness that was excruciating. There were multiple personalities fighting for dominance. God didn't know who or what to trust. Could God trust God's own consciousness? God's existence was like being locked in a padded room with no light. God had all sorts of things in God's mind. God just didn't know what to do with them. There was such a struggle. Sometimes we talk so much that it sounds like there are all types of people around. Did God fight Satan in heaven or was this actually a story of psychological warfare? Maybe Satan is just the name of the mental illness of God. Maybe Satan isn't bad at all. Maybe Satan is just a part of who God is. "Breakdown" is about engaging the eternal problems and afflictions of a mentally ill God before creation.

God is crazy. The breakdown revealed it. Throughout eternity, God just thought that all of the psychosis was normal. Ultimately, God experienced a different revelation. God was sick. God made the decision to seek treatment. Can you imagine what the treatment of God was like? "Treatment" is about a divine diagnosis. God can't grab hold of God's brain. God is desperate for help. God is desperate for light. God is desperate for treatment.

On the first couple of days of creation, God was searching for some serious medicine. The light blended in with the darkness. The water did nothing but dampen God's spirit. The vegetation wouldn't talk back. The heavens just gave God more to worry about. The animals were too busy and made God crazy. When God created humanity, God needed as many people as possible to love God back. God was desperate for love. If God had coerced the love, God wouldn't have experienced real love. Regardless, God was sick and needed something to bring God out of the darkness. For a short time, humans were exactly what the mentally ill God needed. Then, humans made God worse. "Drugs" is an account of the desperate desire of the mentally ill God for a medicine called humans. The creation of humans is an extreme form of psychotropic therapy for God. From the darkness, God was willing to create poison to have a chance at healing. Even though humans are notoriously unreliable and prone to evil, the medicine changed God.

Psychiatric drugs take you for the ride of your life. One might be manic. One might be depressed. One might repeatedly cycle. One might hear voices. One might experience wild mood swings. One might leave the brain behind. One might do all sorts of things. The nature of medicine is that sometimes we don't know what the result is going to be. Medicine is experimental. God certainly did some experimenting when God created us. The Old Testament is a chronicle of God's struggle to adjust to God's new medicine. "Adjustment" is a wrestling with the mentally ill God's struggle between health and insanity in the stories of love and destruction. God is really nuts. The difference between God losing control of God's mind and us losing control of our minds is the size of the consequences. We're still struggling with the consequences of God trying to get right. It's not God's fault. God was just very sick. When you look at all of the terrible shit God did in the Old Testament, you realize God needed more help. God needed the institutionalization of the incarnation.

Was God institutionalized voluntarily or involuntarily? God kept getting worse and worse. The medicine was simply not working. Paralyzed with depression, God couldn't move. Overcome with mania, God couldn't stop causing pain. Voices kept encouraging God to get help. God couldn't move. In the darkness, God considered pulling the plug. God was desperate. Eventually, God willed God's self toward the care that God needed. When God arrived, there was an understanding that this was more than serious. Strapped to a gurney, God's will was all that pushed the wheels down the celestial hallway. God knew what God needed. Over the door, the sign read, "Earth." God knew what the room meant. Thrashing and turning on the gurney, God screamed out in resistance. The doors opened and God pushed through. The next thing God experienced was the shock of the overwhelming smell of shit in a stable in Bethlehem. "Shock" is an interpretation of the incarnation as shock therapy for God. During God's time on earth, one does not have to wonder anymore why God said a few crazy things. God was struggling through every jolt of electricity. The humans were the shock. The experience was poisonous. God was shocked to death. In a desperate moment God opened up God's self to the fullness of human love, the shock of it all brought God back from the dead. Though back, God still needed more.

God's stay in the institution wasn't uneventful. Just because God cheated death doesn't mean that everything was immediately well. God needed more attention. God's mood shifted wildly. There were still voices. God played with humanity to ease God's mind. Sometimes, God made things worse. In an attempt to let humanity experience a little psychosis, God introduced Pentecost. Later, God let a man named John experience some of God's visions. John took it seriously and thought God was talking about the end of the world. Isn't it amazing what can happen when an entity as powerful as God lets others in on their psychosis? "Stay" is a chronicle of a mentally ill God's extended incarnation/institutionalization in the New Testament. Repeatedly, God lets humans journey into God's psychosis. Repeatedly, humans take it further than God ever considered possible. As the story plays out, it's easy to see that God's not the only one suffering from mental illness.

God is mentally ill. From the depths of sickness, God cries out to us. God calls us to engage God's story. God is not alone. The mentally ill call out for us to see God in them. Will we respond to the calls? Will we dare believe that the mentally ill are perfectly made in the image of a mentally ill God? Do not be afraid. God is with us.

Breakdown

"Hear my cry . . ."—Psalm 61:1

BREAKDOWN RAVAGED THE MIND. Before the beginning, there was only fear. Before the beginning, there was only insanity. Before the beginning, there was only longing for the beginning. This is the story of hopelessness. This is the story of chaos. This is the story of mental illness. This is the story of an intervention that led to a beginning. This is the story of God.

War

". . . war broke out in heaven . . ."—Revelation 12:7

"What are you?" "When will you listen to us?" The voices kept whispering. "You are worthless!" "Move!" The voices grew louder and louder. "When are you going to create something out of nothing?" "When are you going to act like God?" The voices screamed. "Do something!" The Holy Trinity is a deficient description of divinity. There were many more than three voices. Grabbing at anything stable, God thrashed around. "I need help!" There was no help to be found for the creator of all that is. The more God called out, the more God was reminded of the hollow echo. Like millions of lightening bolts launched in the same direction at the same time, the echoes kept coming. "Which voices are old?" God wasn't sure. God only knew that they wouldn't stop. "Which voices are new?" God knew that nothing was new. Everything just was.

"I'm here to destroy you." The voice was as evil as anything God had ever heard. "It's time to die." "You should commit suicide." "Don't you know how to do anything right?" Considering the possibilities, God realized that evil was inside the divine mind. "How did it get there?" God couldn't figure anything out. The voices were winning. God couldn't move. God couldn't function. God was totally incapacitated. God hid. God prayed. God cried. Everything remained the same. Fearful of the consequences, God resisted thinking. The darkness grew.

Knowing that God could think God's self out of existence, God wrestled with the thought of annihilation. In the divine mind, the only way to keep something from happening was to hold it closely. God's grip slipped on the thought of embracing annihilation. The grip loosened to a point of holding onto the thought by a string. The string swayed and quivered. If it dropped, God would be no more. While holding the delicate string, God began to think. God thought about how lonely the darkness was. God thought about how much hate God had for God's own brain. God thought about how miserable God was. God thought about the voices and personalities that were constantly with God. In the midst of the thoughts, God decided to let the thought of annihilation drop. Somewhere between existence and annihilation, the breakdown was complete.

Who could fathom the breakdown of God? Even God was unable to imagine what was exploding in the divine mind. Voices, visions, impulses, noises and many other manifestations with and without names refused to stop. Who can comprehend it? Mental illness is beyond all understanding. There is no explaining any of it. Maybe the inability to explain is the greatest evidence that mental illness is inextricably intertwined with God. We cannot explain what is going on in the minds of the afflicted. We cannot explain what is going on in the afflicted mind of God. There is unity in affliction. In the meaninglessness of it all, we find the God in whose image we are made. The only way to gain a glimpse of what God goes through is to look through the breakdowns that surround us to the greatest breakdown that ever was.

"It was the man in the top hat!" Sweat poured from every piece of skin that I owned. As my chest rapidly compressed up and down, I chased my breath but couldn't catch it. The heart was doing things that I never considered possible. The evil voice kept telling me to come back to sleep and play. There has been no voice in my life that has produced more anxiety. The entirety of my physiology was breaking down. Responding to the screams, my parent ran around the corner and said, "Go back to sleep. You were just having a bad dream." Though I tried to tell them, my parents had no way of knowing what was going on. I knew the consequences of closing my eyes. I figured that I could just stay awake. For months I tried to sleep as little as possible, the man in the top hat joined me during the day. I would see him everywhere I went. I would hear him even more. Panic attacks became a daily occurrence. I lived in a perpetual nightmare. Though I tried to talk to many people, no one could help. I was afflicted by delusions by day and nightmares by night.

"Remember me?" Sitting at the bottom of the floor, I looked up. There he was leaning toward me from my television. I dropped my action figures and tried to run. "Don't run! I'm your friend!" Every word revealed razor sharp teeth dripping with blood. With a black and white outfit that looked like something from a hundred years ago, the man drew closer and closer to my face. I knew I was meeting evil. "I want you to join me in here. We'll have so much fun." I was paralyzed. Though I wanted to scream, I couldn't do anything. I just kept opening and closing my eyes. No matter what I did, the face of evil was still there in front of mine. "Why don't you go get your dad's gun? You can suck on it like a lollipop and pull the trigger." I started praying as hard as I could. I was terrified. Physiologically, I knew that I was in the full throes of a breakdown. Though I didn't call it that then, I knew that there were times when I lost control of my entire being and felt like I was being choked to death by hopelessness. On that day, I remembered a part of a verse I learned at church, " . . . I am with you always . . ." By the time my brother walked in, I was pale. Can you imagine sleeping next to the television later that night? I just tried to remember that God was experiencing everything with me.

Everything was on the brink of collapse. Light collapsed into darkness and darkness collapsed into light. The spirit of the man in the top hat led to a great disruption in the light. God couldn't sleep. Nightmares followed God everywhere. The voice of annihilation repeated over and over. Everywhere God looked the pain increased. The divine heart exploded. The divine mind choked. The divine sweat poured. God prayed for it to end. Knowing God needed something stronger, God began to dream. The problem was that the nightmares mingled with dreams and the dreams mingled with the nightmares to create a space where nothing is real and everything is real. The man with the top hat was the most real unreal experience that God ever had. Fearing that the expansion of evil would lead to the destruction of all that is, God prayed for the end. It came. In the end was the beginning and in the beginning was the end.

"The stage lights are on!" Everyone was whispering in expectation. Not Maggie. In the throes of a panic attack, Maggie was having trouble standing up. Everyone else was so excited. Refusing to let the anxiety keep her from her dreams, Maggie signed up for a solo in her school's choral concert. "Maggie, it's time." The curtain was drawn. Journeying to the middle of stage, Maggie performed her breathing technique over and over. The moment was rapidly approaching. Nothing seemed to be working. "Ladies and gentleman!" The curtain was going to open at any moment. Paralyzed in fear, Maggie could feel her entire body shutting down. The curtain swung open faster than she anticipated. The faces only made everything worse. Was everyone laughing at her? Would she be able to sing the song? Would someone rush the stage and kill her? Would the lights collapse? The endless questions of a young anxious mind repeatedly brutalized her physiology. The complete breakdown arrived. Urine splashed to the floor. Maggie's body collapsed. The curtain was quickly drawn. Paramedics rushed the stage. Regardless of her physical constitution, Maggie was never going to be ok.

Light kept streaking at the face of God. It was all happening too fast. Though God signed up for the moment, it was too much.

Realizing that the time was here, God stepped out into eternity and tried to remain calm. Divine anxiety was crushing parts of the light. God was afraid. The unknown ripped light from light. Could God do it? Could God be God? What if God wasn't up to the task? What if light collapsed? What if God failed? Seeking a way out, God reached for annihilation. Pulling back, God collapsed. There was no one to help. There was no one to care. Something had to change. Regardless of God's ability to survive, God was never going to be ok.

Thrashing under the weight of it all, Harvey kept thrashing back and forth. One could almost see the adrenaline rushing through his body. The paramedics immediately regretted putting him into the ambulance. One of the paramedics took a kick to the face and slammed into the cabinets. Glass crashed to the floor. Harvey kept screaming. One of the paramedics gave him a shot to tranquilize him. The powerful concoction didn't work. Thinking that he was in a battle with the forces of evil, Harvey was giving it all that he had. As far as the entirety of Harvey was concerned, the fate of the world depended on it. Arriving at the hospital, Harvey was placed in a padded room. Unable to get out, Harvey just kept fighting. Everyone who came in contact with Harvey thought he was on some powerful drugs. When the blood tests came back, the doctors realized that he was mentally ill and suffering from powerful delusions. After some time, Harvey collapsed into a fetal position in the corner. Shaking for hours, Harvey realized that he needed help sorting out what was going on in his body. For the first time, Harvey decided that he needed strong medication. The end of the breakdown led to a new creation.

"Get back!" Convinced that a battle between good and evil was raging, God slung light everywhere. Thrashing back and forth, God was full of destruction. When anything tried to help, God sought to destroy them. God could not be contained. Everything crashed. Everything shattered. Everything was broken. God was prepared to destroy it all. Eternity hung in the balance. God oscillated between tears and rage. Could anyone understand what was going on in the divine mind? Could anyone help? God was so afflicted. God was so alone. God collapsed and shuttered in the darkness. God was so broken. God knew that more was needed. Who could help? God couldn't function. God hated the thought of needing help. God was supposed to be God right? God fell hard. God landed flat. God felt crushed. The weight finally brought total destruction. God wondered if it was over. Passing out, God thought annihilation was finally here. There was no one to come to God's aid. "Please help me!" The last thought God had before it was over was one of creation. The end of the breakdown was a new beginning.

Intervention
"...from where will my help come from?"—Psalm 121:1

"Will you help me?" Who was God talking to? Was the voice divine? Was the voice coming from within? Was the voice coming from somewhere else? Who could help? Before long, God realized that the voice was divine. For the first time, God sought professional help. This was the biggest decision God ever made. Fear was not going to stop God this time. The consequences of divine determination changed eternity. Sitting down, God was told that God was very ill. "Without medication, you will eventually annihilate God." God didn't have to be convinced how serious everything was. God felt every piece of the diagnosis. God was ready to embrace whatever treatment was needed.

Opening the glass door, John walked into a room full of fake trees. Each one had those waxy leaves that collect dust better than any cleaning agent ever could. Taking a seat, John prayed his allergies wouldn't flare up. The smell was nauseating. "Who puts this much air freshener in any room?" Repeatedly, John considered walking out. Fear was a constant presence in that lonely waiting room. "No one will ever know." Love kept John from moving. Refusing to be moved, John repeatedly rubbed his hands. The skin was already scared with red and inflamed sores. This was not the first time he'd spent an extended amount of time anxiously rubbing his hands. The door swung open. "John!" The time had come. Barely able to move, John slowly and nervously walked back to the office. Sitting down, the doctor tried to assure John that she was going to get him the help that he needed. John couldn't handle it and got up to leave. The thought of his kids pushed him back to the chair. Due to the records he brought with him, the doctor was very aware of his condition. "How have you survived so long without treatment?" The question only reminded John of how much needed help. After a long uncomfortable conversation, the doctor was ready to prescribe treatment. Sweat poured from his body. Unable to deal with the uncertainty of the moment, John only knew to expect the worst.

God opened the door. How could the creator of all that is or will ever be need treatment for mental illness? The waiting was terrible. God kept thinking about walking out. "I don't really need any help." The divine mind knew better. Thinking about all the thoughts of annihilation that plagued his brain, God kept returning to the seat. "I need help." Growing impatient, God kept wondering about how long he'd been forced to sit there. Though sick, the divine mind knew that leaving would only make things worse. The space was closing in. Sweat was pouring. The ceiling was going to collapse at any moment. God kept rubbing anxious sores on the divine body. The space grew hotter by the second. The divine stomach was about to explode. God was struggling mightily right there in the lobby. The door swung open. "God!" The time had arrived. When God attempted to stand, the divine legs gave out. Help came from everywhere. The doctor led the patient back. Lying on the exam table, God started to calm down. Thoughts of the future helped. Leaning in, the doctor assured God that all was going to be ok. For an extended amount of time, God told the doctor all that was wrong. "How long have you been experiencing these symptoms?" "Eternity." Unable to comprehend why it took God so long to seek treatment, the doctor assured God that this was the best decision the divine mind had ever made. After both sweat and tears dripped to the floor, the doctor was prepared to prescribe treatment. The uncertainty of the moment was excruciating. God prayed that the great physician really would be great.

"I can't breathe." Those were the only words that Rebecca could manage. With his head in his hands, Rebecca cried behind the clothes. Society pushed her to the back of the closet. No one could get her out. "Rebecca, we love you!" Even the pleas of a few friends didn't seem to be making any difference. The hold of the depression was too strong. Pain has a way of sending us to places that we didn't even know were possible. Depression slowly choked out all life. Late one night, Rebecca collapsed. Early the next morning, Rebecca's friends discovered Rebecca without a pulse. The group immediately started CPR. When paramedics arrived, they refused to touch her. "Any man who wears lipstick and a dress has to have communicable diseases! We can't work on him. It's against our religion." Instead of debating, Rebecca's friends rushed Rebecca to the hospital in the closest large city. Emergency room doctors saved her life. Coming out into the waiting room, the doctors used technical language to declare that Rebecca was suffering from a broken heart caused by excruciating oppression and marginalization. Returning to the room, the doctors prepared to share with Rebecca their plan for her treatment. Rebecca was angry that mental illness brought on by the pain of an evil society was forcing her to need treatment.

God was trapped in a closet of oppression. Tears rained down. God retreated further. Nothing could open the door. The depression was too strong. God was an outcast. Excruciating loneliness choked off any chance of recovery. "How did this happen? I can't move. I can't think. I can't breathe." God collapsed under the weight of it all. There was no one there to help. Declining rapidly, God just tried to hold on. When help did arrive, God was forced to endure the pain of their bullying and hate. Realizing that God might not make it, doctors rushed to save God. The diagnoses came swiftly. God was suffering from loneliness and depression brought on by marginalization and oppression. The doctors were ready to share their prescribed treatment plan. God was still angry that mental illness was pushed upon the divine mind in the first place. God wanted a cure and no cure was ever going to be available.

Beginning
"In the beginning . . ."—Genesis 1:1

The breakdown led to a moment of intervention. These moments are always unexpected. These moments are always unwelcome. These moments are always difficult. Between the intervention and the treatment lies a beginning. The mentally ill are able to begin anew when the breakdown creates an intervention that creates a future. We are not the first to walk these crazy paths. God needed intervention too. The divine treatment created something new . . . something in the beginning.

Treatment

"... rescue me ..."—Psalm 31:2

NOTHING PREPARES YOU FOR treatment. The fear you face stepping into the unknown is unparalleled. During the breakdown, you could rely on the fact that everything was going to be chaos. Numbness becomes a friend. Pain becomes a partner. Confusion becomes clarity. During the treatment, you don't know what any of it will be like. You only know that you will experience something new. Desperation creates a willingness to try anything. God knows desperation. God knows treatment. God knows prescription. God knows the struggle.

Prescription
"Deliver me ..."—Psalm 140:1

"I need help." Three words changed everything. God was finally exposed. The lie of perfection would be no more. Terror gripped the divine heart. "How can I be God when my condition makes me not God?" The voices kept chanting for God's demise. Anxiety filled every moment. Exposure was the enemy of God. If it became known that God was anything other than perfect, the game was up. "I've got to get out of here." Something kept God seated in that room. Something kept God from the door. Something caused God to long for a new beginning. Though the voices kept telling God to leave, God refused to believe the voices. "Help is an illusion." The voices were so strong that they seemed to be controlling the divine brain. Finally with all of the strength that God muster, God screamed out, "Stop!" The door swung open. Sitting in the darkness, God realized that the prescription was ready. The conversation centered on God's hopelessness and the voices. In order to be rescued, God had to create the rescuers. The only way to be God is to create in God's image. In order to be God, you have to give God away. The mental illness would continue. There would be no cure. Creation could only treat the most extreme symptoms. In the coldness of the prescription, God had to decide whether compliance was divine.

In the midst of a wild brain, church was always a source of hope for Gerald. The colors helped him to dream. The sounds helped him to love. The symbols helped him to think. Since he was a child, Gerald loved church. Even though Gerald was one of the most consistent members, no one knew that Gerald struggled with problems in his brain. One day after a particularly spiritual sermon, Gerald decided to make an appointment with his pastor. Even though the fear, anxiety and voices told him not to, Gerald felt that now was the time to get help. Entering the pastor's office, Gerald screamed out, "My brain is sick!" Though he didn't believe in taking medication for mental issues, the pastor offered to excise Gerald's head. In the midst of the wild prayer, Gerald had a severe attack. Sweat poured profusely. Gerald's entire body shook. Urine trickled down his leg. Sensing he had the demon on the run, the pastor pushed Gerald further. Right at the climax of the shouting and shaking, Gerald collapsed and stopped breathing. Realizing that he'd made a big mistake, the pastor called an ambulance. On the way to the hospital, Gerald was revived. After a few hours of treatment, doctors informed Gerald that he was going to have to start taking medicine for his brain. Gerald told the doctors that it was against his religion. "If you want to live and avoid what happened today, you need to take this medicine." When his pastor suggested that they pray further, Gerald started experiencing another attack. After the room was cleared, Gerald was left with the question of compliance.

There was nowhere else to go. God dropped to the floor. Spirituality was the only place of solace God could find. Sometimes God worried that God spent too much time in prayer. Then, God continuously prayed about it and decided against it. From the floor, God tried to counsel God's self. "Are all the voices demons? Am I the demon?" Rolling around, God was very confused. When God started having visions of evil, God screamed out, "My mind is sick!" Though God was scared to take anything for the illness that afflicted the divine mind, God was getting increasingly desperate. In the midst of praying about what to do, God started having an attack. Every piece of God started to explode. God thought it was over. Thankfully, the light saved God. When the diagnosis came, all that God feared finally came to pass. God needed some type of medication. Though it was against everything God believed, God started to lean toward creating a prescription to get a grip on the divine mind.

"Why do you keep buying books?" Everyone asked me the same question. I didn't respond. I just kept on buying. Books were the only things on my mind. Truthfully, browsing and picking out titles became my medicine. For the first time, I received some relief from the anxiety and depression. I couldn't stop. Few people understand physiologically not being able to stop doing something. "Please stop!" I heard it over and over. When I received the largest bill I'd ever received for anything, I knew I had a problem. I hadn't known until the bill. "I need help." After prayer about what to do next, I decided to make an appointment with my pastor. Repeatedly, my pastor described my condition as the sin of gluttony. "You are definitely sick. You are sin sick. Don't go to a psychiatrist! They will just drug you up and you'll never be the same! Turn to God!" By the end of the meeting, I was struggling with what to do. During the prayer, the anxiety took over. I opened my computer to buy more books. I had to stop. The next morning, I made an appointment with the psychiatrist. Even though I was terrified, I couldn't get there fast enough. Greeting me with a smile, my doctor spoke very soothing words, "Do not be afraid! I am here to help." Slightly calmer, I descended into the big leather chair and told her about my life. After several tests and hours of conversation, my psychiatrist replied, "You are one of the worst cases I've ever seen go so long without treatment." It was nice to know that I was crazy. I knew a big struggle for me was coming up. I'd prayed about it ever since I decided to make an appointment. "I'm going to prescribe you . . ." For most of my life, I'd believed that mental illness wasn't real. I'd believed that mental difficulties were the result of sin. I'd believed that medication was a tool of the devil to keep you from dealing with real problems. I'd believed . . . I had to choose not to believe. After the psychiatrist called in the prescription, I asked her to pray with me about taking the medicine. Though of another religion, she didn't hesitate. The psychiatrist displayed the love of God far more than my pastor did. When I arrived at the drugstore and picked up my medication, I pulled out a pill. I sat there for a long time trying to decide whether I would take it or not.

God acted impulsively. Wild urges controlled everything about God. Instead of responding to the questions in the divine mind, God kept responding to the impulses. God just kept doing it over and over. Impulses became the medicine of God. By follow-ing the divine impulses, God was experiencing some relief from mental illness for the first time in all of eternity. "Please stop!" God repeatedly heard the same phrase. Voices in the divine mind kept telling God that the impulses were evil. Other voices told God that the impulses were good. "I don't know who to believe!" When God destroyed a significant amount of light, God realized that God had a problem. Fearful of any type of medication, God resisted trying to examine the divine mind. When God's impulses kept destroying the light, God realized that it was necessary. Opening up the mind, God couldn't believe how bad it was. The divine mind was ravaged with sickness. God began to panic. Anxiety took over. God seized on the floor. Within the divine mind, God heard a voice declare, "I am here to help you." Returning to the divine mind, God realized for the first time in God's existence that God was crazy. Listening to the voice, God decided that it was time to start medication. In the midst of eternity, God had to dream up the prescription.

Though medication is a common form, there are many ways to treat mental illness. Some pursue the route of psychology. Some turn to spiritual solutions. Some chose natural remedies. Some find other solutions. Still others create their own solutions by piecing a bunch of different therapies together. In the midst of struggling with mental illness, God asked the same question we all do, "What is the healthiest decision for me?" In the midst of the initial struggle for some level of healing, God chose the meds.

Pills

". . . a very present help in trouble."—Psalm 46:1

Most people who are mentally ill are hesitant to embrace medication. Most sufferers realize that medication is a game you're never going to win. Regardless of what you take, there are always negative physical consequences. Those who start medication often become dependent on the medication. No one wants to have to take pills the rest of their lives. Unfortunately, medication is the only path to any quality of life for most sufferers. God knows the difficulty of the decision. God is suffering. God is experiencing the pain of mental illness. God is struggling through the process of treatment. Those who disparage medication as a solution to the suffering of the mentally ill do not know God.

In the examination room, God wrestled with the decision. The realization that treatment would lead to a new creation weighed heavily on God. "Am I prepared for something radically different? Am I prepared to change? What if the medication doesn't work?" The questions raced through every corner of the divine mind. Newness is always terrifying. God didn't know what was coming next. God didn't know what could be. God only knew what was. In the midst of the terror of the present, God had to figure something out. The doctor returned and handed God a prescription. "Your mental illness will kill you unless you take something. You can't continue going on like this." God wasn't sure if something was talking to him. God wasn't sure if anything was actually there. Regardless of what was real, God had to do something. Opening the divine hand, God stared at the pills. Everything in the heart of God said to crush the pills. Everything in the divine mind said to drop the pills. Everything begged God not to take the pills. Everything was a liar. In the midst of the struggle, God started to realize that God needed this. God needed help. Raising the pills to the divine mouth, God leaned back, tossed them in and swallowed. A new creation arrived immediately.

Metal crushed. Glass shattered. Sounds exploded. The damage was severe. As the smoke slowly cleared, someone approached the car and said, "Are you ok?" Marissa was going in and out. The impact alone was enough to make anyone's consciousness a little foggy. By the time the paramedics arrived, Marissa was still not awake. Even in her unconscious state, she could still feel the anxiety. Marissa's entire nervous system was firing off repeatedly. When the paramedics strapped her to the gurney, Marissa felt like she was under attack. A few minutes into the ride, Marissa came to and tried to get off the stretcher. The paramedics encouraged her to remain flat. Looking down, Marissa could see her entire skeleton shaking. The accident made the anxiety worse. Panic attacks riddled her body. Racing toward the hospital, the paramedics monitored her heart. Upon her arrival at the hospital, Marissa was sedated. When Marissa's parents entered the hospital room, they knew. For weeks, they'd encouraged her to get treatment for her anxiety. Feeling like medication would take something away from her, Marissa resisted. When she finally came to at the hospital, the doctor entered the room. "Your anxiety is not just a threat to you. You're anxiety is a threat to everyone. Your anxiety caused the accident this morning. You need to be medicated." After laying out her treatment regiment, the doctor left the initial dose with her. For over an hour, Marissa looked at the pills. Knowing that the pills would change her life, she resisted. Marissa didn't want things to be new. Marissa wanted things to stay the same. The anxiety told her to stay away from the pills. The anxiety told her that the pills would take away her edge. The anxiety told her to throw the pills away. Marissa knew that the anxiety was a liar. After a brief pause to breathe, Marissa got a cup of water, raised them to her mouth and swallowed the pills. Immediately, Marissa created something new.

Light crashed. Consciousness shattered. Colors exploded. Sounds burst. The damage was great. As the smoke slowly cleared, God heard a voice say, "Are you ok?" Going in and out, God couldn't reply. The impact alone could have destroyed God. When help arrived, God felt like it was an attack. Even in an unconscious state, God felt the anxiety of it all. When God came to, God was shaking all over. Fighting all help, God couldn't stop shivering. The accident made the anxiety worse. Panic attacks kept hitting. God couldn't figure out where God was. God desperately needed help. Throughout eternity, God refused help. Now, God knew the game was up. Something had to change. The doctor entered the room and said, "Your anxiety is the single greatest threat ever. You need to be medicated before you cause another accident." After laying out the treatment plan, the doctor left the initial dose of medication on the table. God refused to turn the divine eyes away from the pills. Afraid, God resisted. Knowing that the pills would greatly change the divine mind, God pushed back. The wrestling was eternal. The anxiety was dangerous. The anxiety could lead to annihilation. The anxiety could ruin everything. The anxiety told God to run. The anxiety called God worthless. The anxiety was trapped in the divine mind. The anxiety never told the truth. God reached for the pills. After swallowing all of them, God created something new.

Running wildly around the village, Elijah repeatedly screamed, "The sky is falling!" No one knew what to do. One of the local pastors tackled Elijah. While holding him to the ground, the pastor performed an exorcism. Villagers rushed to help. After tying Elijah to a tree, the pastor led the villagers to scream and spit at him. Throughout the ordeal, Elijah kept screaming, "The sky is falling!" Eventually, Elijah was rendered unconscious. People got tired of trying to excise someone possessed by unresponsive demons. Under the cover of night, Elijah's friends loaded him into a truck and drove him to the closest hospital. Following an extended amount of time, Elijah saw a doctor. Immediately, the doctor recognized a serious case of mental illness. After many hours of tests, the doctor returned and told Elijah that he would need to go on medication. Throughout his life, Elijah was told that medicine was a tool of the devil. Elijah suspected that what he was seeing might not be real. Desperate to not be controlled, Elijah asked for medication. When the pills arrived, Elijah raced to them. Despite his hesitancies and fear, Elijah picked the pills up and swallowed them. Immediately, Elijah was a new creation.

Running around the heavens, God loudly screamed, "The end is near! The end is near! The end is near!" God didn't know what to do. The divine mind was uncontrollable. Something jumped at God. Something screamed at God. Something tackled God. Throughout the ordeal, God kept screaming, "The end is near!" After the screaming and spitting ended, God was motionless. Eventually, doctors came to the aid of God. Dragging God to an exam room, the doctors revived God. After going over God's history and current practices, the doctors diagnosed God with a severe case of mental illness. Medication would be necessary. When the doctors returned with the divine prescription, God hesitated. "Why should the sustainer of all that is or will ever be need medication?" Pride forced God to sit there thinking for a long time. When the pills arrived, God looked at them. One by one, God picked them up and studied them. Eventually, God swallowed them. Creation came next.

Light
" . . . Let there be light . . ."—Genesis 1:3

Prescriptions are a result of seeking treatment. God had the courage to seek treatment. Medications are a result of prescriptions. God found the courage to engage medication. Medications lead to creation or new life. You cannot take medication or follow a prescribed plan of treatment without things becoming different than what they were before. God took the pills and things became different. Creation blossomed out of the mind of God. Following the first few creative thoughts, God wanted to do something about the darkness and said, "Let there be light . . ." After turning on the lights, God was ready for the greatest act of creation yet . . . a medicine called humanity.

Drugs

"Let us make humankind in our own image . . ."—Genesis 1:26

TREATMENT ALWAYS LEADS TO something new. Our world changes as we change. Medications shock the system. It takes time to understand whether the medication is working or not. Sometimes the medications fail. Sometimes we have to change medications. Sometimes we have to change dosages. Sometimes we have to add medications. Sometimes we have to change when we take the medications. God kept pushing us through the process. There are millions of different of paths in the journey toward a healthier mind. God took them all. Suffering from all types of sicknesses and disorders, God started to refer to God's self using all sorts of names and imagery. God desperately needed help. Before arriving at the pills, God's treatment led to the creation of all sorts of things. When we don't get it right, we have to keep trying until we get it close to right. After many different attempts, humanity was the closest thing to right treatment that God found. Humans were the pills that God needed. Things got crazier from there.

Attempts

"And God said . . ."—Genesis 1:6

" . . . Let there be light . . ." (1:3). God knew light before, but God needed a greater light. In the midst of unbelievable depression, God took the pill of light and separated the light from the darkness. The problem was that light didn't do anything for the mania.

Truth be told, it only made things worse. Though God felt energized, God had no ability to control the energy. The hyperactivity was frightening. Desperate to stop the sensation, God tried another type of medication.

The new pills did a number on me. I'd never liked comic books before. One day, I saw a comic book shop and had to stop. Before I knew it, I was picking up everything in the store. I loved the colors. I couldn't get enough of them. The mania spread to every one of my senses. I wanted to see the comics. I wanted to smell the comics. I wanted to be the comics. I even nibbled a piece of one comic book just to see what it tasted like. I was so happy. Throwing my hands into the air, I screamed, "Let there be comic books!" The colors separated the light from darkness. The problem was that I couldn't control the energy. There had to be another way. I decided to take a different medication.

" . . . let it seperate . . ." (1:6). God struggled with the polarities of mania and depression. Throughout eternity, God had no concept of anything between. God needed balance yet yearned for the mania. The only way to get the extreme highs was to also embrace the extreme lows. However, the extreme lows were drowning God. When the depression lasted much longer than God anticipated, God took the pill of between. For a moment, God felt better. God was just happy to let go of the depression. Unfortunately, it wasn't long before God felt stuck between. The highs were gone. The lows were gone. There was only mediocre. There was only stability. There was only that place where things expire. Desperate to move beyond between, God tried another type of medication.

The art was amazing. No one had ever seen such creativity. When Jennifer was manic, she produced some of the most spectacular work imaginable. When Jennifer was depressed, she couldn't even get out of bed. Unwilling to sacrifice her creativity for sanity, Jennifer just produced as much art as she could while she was manic. During one brutal stretch, Jennifer couldn't take the depression any more. Turning to mood stabilizers, Jennifer rushed to a place she'd never known before . . . between. For a few days, between wasn't so bad. After some time went by, between felt like a prison. There were no brilliant periods of creativity. There was no fast production of beauty. Forget about the depression, the mania was gone. Without the mania, Jennifer felt totally tranquilized. Unable to go on, Jennifer decided she had to try something else to save her existence. Between wasn't going to work. Desperate to move beyond stabilization, Jennifer tried another type of medication.

" . . . let the dry land appear . . ." (1:9). God's head was up in the clouds. Thoughts and emotions were difficult to find. Feeling like an aimless balloon, God was desperate for anything that would bring order to the divine mind. God felt like he'd moved beyond the other ailments. The problem was that the medicines now made God feel like he couldn't do anything. God didn't want to trade one ailment for another. Desperate for control, God gave up on the other medications. Everything that had afflicted God came crashing back. The mania. The depression. The voices. The confusion. Thinking it might take some time to get beyond the former ailments, God waited. Even though things got worse, God still waited. Instead of floating, God was now getting beat back and forth by unnamed forces in the air. Sensing that things were not going to get better, God tried another type of medication.

"What is wrong with you? Get your head out of the clouds!" Unable to control his thoughts, Juan felt like he floated through life. Relationships disintegrated. School was impossible. Driving down the street was difficult. Nobody wanted to help. In his small community, people had two explanations for mental illness: demon possession or drugs. For many years, people thought Juan was on drugs. "We can provide you help with your addiction." Unfortunately, the answers to Juan's problems were different than the common offer for help. There were no mental health services in town. People assumed that mental illness was an excuse for demon possession or drug use. There were no legitimate offers for real help. Regardless of external events, Juan's mind just floated aimlessly. Occasionally things got worse, on these days Juan felt like his mind was tied to a string tied to a pole and being beaten around by a tennis racket. During one particularly bad experience, Juan tried an herbal remedy for confusion. Things just got worse. Juan sent an email to a doctor a few towns over. The doctor encouraged Juan to come to his office immediately. Though everything in his mind told him not to, Juan did. Floating through life wasn't going to work anymore. Desperate to come back down to the ground and realizing that everything else wasn't working, Juan was ready to try a different type of medication.

" . . . let them be for signs and for seasons and for days and years." (1:14). The mundane took over. There was no difference between anything. Everything remained the same. The highs were no more. The lows were no more. Grey was the forever color. Life was stable and safe. God hated it. The medicine destroyed life by neutralizing it. Voices still taunted God. The only difference was that they spoke as slow as life took place. God was paralyzed. Afraid that nothing would ever change again, God reached out for the pill of change. Things began to move. Things began to change.

Robert was all over the place. Unable to gain any grip on his mind, Robert regularly lost control. Robert wasn't violent often. Even though he was sometimes wild, people loved Robert and wanted to be around him. For many who knew him, Robert was the light of their life. Unfortunately, Robert had one particularly bad night. Walking home from the bar, Robert decided to rip all of his clothes off and run out into traffic. Robert shook his man parts at every passing car. When the police arrived, Robert felt like he was under attack. Fighting like this fight would be his last, Robert knocked out two police officers. When a group of police officers finally tackled him, Robert farted in one officer's face so hard that he sharted (shit/farted). The police were not happy and roughed him up pretty bad. Eventually, the judge ordered Robert to go on medication. The pills made Robert mundane and controllable. Over time, Robert lost all of his friends. The light was gone. No one cared about spending time with a Robert under control. One friend did stay and convinced Robert to get on a medication that allowed for change. After much persuasion, Robert agreed. The mundane was replaced with color. Unfortunately, the color was just not as vibrant as the color had once been. Though the feelings of change were good, but Robert still missed pieces of the old

Robert. Robert missed life. Going back to the doctor, Robert was ready to try a different type of medication.

" . . . Let the earth bring forth living creatures of every kind . . ." (1:24). The new changes tossed God around. Unprepared for the shifting, God struggled to get a grip. God realized that change just for the sake of change is never worth it. There was a need for substantial change. There was a need for change with life. Though substantially better, God needed more than just change. God needed life. There had to be a better medication.

"Don't touch me." Pat trembled in the corner. Refusing to eat or sleep, Pat grew worse. Unable to ascertain what was real or not, Pat was afraid of everything. In the midst of the worst mental health crises she'd ever faced, Pat fought the entire world. Fighting was the only thing she knew. Pat's friends conspired to get her to the doctor. On the way, Pat woke up violently and caused them to wreck. At the hospital, security had to strap her down to a chair. Doctors immediately tranquilized Pat. After a few days, Pat returned to a positive state. The new medication helped. By the time she was discharged, Pat didn't want to fight anymore. Though better, Pat felt like the medication produced changes but not life. Returning to the doctor a few months later, Pat asked for medication that would bring about substantial change. Pat wanted more than stability. Pat wanted life.

" . . . Let us make humankind in our image . . ." (1:26). God felt better. Switching and changing medications so many times takes a toll. For eternity, God waited on the medications to level out and sometimes to even exit the divine system. When the point arrived for everything to work correctly, God still felt a little off. Health is about arriving at a place of thriving. There are many ways to get there. Unfortunately, some don't have all the tools they need to get there. It's like striving over and over again and repeatedly getting knocked back over and over again. Often, the knocking is painful. Often, the knocking is not. Regardless of how you get knocked, you are still not able to get to the point that you want to be. God knew this feeling well. God experienced getting knocked back to eternity. God needed something else to survive. God needed something else to thrive. God needed more life. God needed the right medication.

Though she'd been taking different medication for many years, Rigoberta was unable to thrive. The medications would level out and leave her needing something else. Even after finding a medication that worked really well, Rigoberta still felt off. Switching medications is exhausting. Instead of going through the process again, Rigoberta decided to just stick with what she had for a little while. Not thriving is much better than dying. Over and over again, Rigoberta got knocked back. She just didn't have what she needed to thrive. After a particularly disturbing day, Rigoberta decided that she was tired of the dull pain. Making an appointment with her doctor, Rigoberta was ready for something more. Believing that it existed, Rigoberta kept pushing. When she arrived in the office, Rigoberta expressed her inability to thrive on all the medications that she'd been on before. "I want to be more creative." The doctor understood. Leaning in, the doctor handed her a medication that he thought was created just for her. "This will give you an ability to experience an existence fuller then you ever dreamed possible. The rest is up to you."

Medicine
". . . in the image of God . . ."—Genesis 1:27

"I need something more." In the search for right treatment, God experienced all different types of new creation. The light didn't help with the depression. The between just took away life. The ground made God feel like a zombie wondering through existence. The change led to violence. The new life made God more stable. The light battled depression. The between battled bipolar. The ground battled schizophrenia. The change battled God's catatonic state. The new life battled dementia. There are many names and descriptions for what God was experiencing. Any one diagnosis is rarely able to completely describe what is going on in any sufferer. Multiple diagnoses were unable to describe what God was going through. God suffers from everything. Each treatment brought on new troubles and new creation. God was very sick and growing sicker. No medicine seemed to alleviate the divine mind. Desperate, God tried one more.

Humans were made in God's image. God was able to fully engage with something else. God didn't have to suffer alone. God was able to love for the first time. God didn't have to talk to the voices. God could talk to real people with their own voices. Humans brought God a profound sense of responsibility. The human medicine helped God regulate the divine mind. God didn't have to live solely in the divine mind anymore. God could live amongst the living. God could be whole. God could dance with others. God could sing with others. God could laugh with others. God could create with others. The human medicine was strong enough to treat all of God's ailments. For the first time, God was thriving.

Over the years, I tried many different types of medicine. The first one made me manic all the time. I felt like Superman. I thought this was the way I was supposed to feel all the time. I couldn't believe what I'd been missing out on. Everything was great until things got crazy. I tried to cut down a tree at my grandparent's house in the middle of the night. I bought a bunch of stuff. I ran around naked in strange places. I got in fights. The medication didn't work. The second one was more of a sedative. I was a zombie. During a wedding, I collapsed. On another night/day, I didn't wake up for almost 20 hours straight. While I missed feeling like Superman, I knew I didn't want to feel like this. The third one made me hallucinate. I started seeing all sorts of things. You want your medicine to make your hallucinations lessen not increase. I moved on. The fourth one stabilized my mind. After being on it for a few weeks, I told my doctor that I knew that this was the substance my body always needed. I learned to be back amongst the living. I learned to be whole again. I learned to dance. I learned to sing. I learned to laugh. I learned to create. The medicine was strong enough to treat my afflictions. For the first time, I was thriving.

Filling

"... another account ..."—Genesis 2:4

How does God fill a prescription? The process is always difficult. When you're God, it's not difficult to think about and diagnose your problems. It's difficult to seek treatment. It's impossible to fill the prescription. God can easily dream up and test medications. God can figure out plans of treatment. The problem is that God can't stick to them. God is perpetually frightened of new medication. On far too many occasions, the medication went wrong. When the medication goes wrong, eternity hangs in the balance. Filling the medication is about weighing the cost. Before the moment that changed everything forever, God sat in the heavenly realm. Deeply troubled about what to do next, God stared at the prescription. Anxiety crashed against anxiety. Depression drowned depression. Voices talked over voices. Hallucinations competed for attention. Mania sped up. God hated medication. The problem was that God felt like the divine mind was going to explode. After five recent unsuccessful attempts at medications, God felt trapped in a vortex of confusion and wild emotions. Swept around the celestial realm, God held tight to the prescription. In the midst of the chaos, God thought about the needs of the divine mind. Not wanting to go on another medication, God struggled over and over. Eventually, God grabbed the divine head and rushed to fill the prescription. Nothing would ever be the same.

Emily couldn't fill that damn prescription. Throughout her life, Emily was told that sin was the reason for her mental problems. Why couldn't she just pray to make the problems go away? Why couldn't she just read her Bible more? Why couldn't she just .. .? Everyone at church looked down on her. If Emily got unsolicited counsel from five concerned people not to go to the doctor, she got it from a hundred. "Just trust God." "There's nothing wrong with you that a little prayer can't fix." "I don't believe in mental illness." "God is the great physician." "No man will want to have anything to do with you if they think you're crazy." The comments were endless. Though Emily tried to resist, many of the comments hit her at her core. When Emily finally decided to go to the doctor, she told no one. Leaving under the cover of the early morning darkness, Emily drove many miles to a bigger city. The waiting room was terrifying. After multiple tests and extended conversation, the doctor diagnosed Emily and gave her a prescription for some medicine that would level her out. The only problem was that there was only one pharmacy within a hundred miles of the small town she lived in. Everyone would know that she was taking medication. Determined to get better, Emily drove home. Fear increased with every mile. The blue and white sign loomed in the distance. Swerving into the parking lot, Emily took the fateful walk to the back. When Emily presented the prescription, the pharmacist reminded her that these were powerful drugs for people with very serious mental disorders. Emily tried to block it all out. By the time the prescription was filled, the pharmacist had called Emily's parents. Before she ever took the medicine, Emily was kicked out of her house and church. Who would've thought that filling a prescription could change life so dramatically?

Taking
"... God took the ..."—Genesis 2:15

Medications are not easy to take. Most pills don't come in chewable forms. This is true both literally and metaphorically. In a literal sense, pills make you gag. Depending on the size, pills might even make you puke all over the place. Gagging and puking doesn't sound like a pleasant experience. In a metaphorical sense, the pills are a regular reminder that the taker is crazy. Who needs a constant reminder that they're deficient? You also don't know what the pills are going to do. You're taking a risk every time you force one down your throat. Knowing that you might be swallowing your own demise is a tough pill to swallow. Medications are not often chewable. God knows it too.

"How am I supposed to swallow these gigantic pills?" God was incredulous. Despite knowing that the pills were exactly what God needed, God couldn't stomach the thought of actually taking them. " I thought medication was supposed to make you feel better?" The sight of the pills made God feel worse. Picking the pills up, God tried to swallow one. God gagged until celestial puke sprayed all over the place. "Isn't there an easier way to do this?" The medication was humanity. The dosage was all of it. There was no other way. Humanity didn't come in a chewable form. Humanity had to be swallowed. God realized that something in the divine mind was blocking the medication. Up until now, God thought of this as just a little problem. Now, the medication forced God to realize something more . . . that God was crazy and always would be. Leaning back, God picked up humanity and forced them down the divine throat. Instantly, it happened. "Oh my God!" A new creation exploded before the divine eyes.

"I don't even want to look at those damn things!" Scott's struggle with the trauma led him to seek treatment. The bravado that carried Scott through life was inhibiting him from actually taking the pills that were prescribed to him. The room was a mess. On the table, there was a pistol and a pill. Both options were tough to chew on. "If I blow my damn brains out, I won't have any brains to worry about." Time helped Scott lean toward the only sensible option. First, Scott would have to swallow the pills. Gagging repeatedly, Scott finally got one down. With watery eyes, Scott declared victory. With the first swallow, Scott realized that he was officially crazy. In the midst of the pain of what that might mean, Scott had the most brilliant sensation he'd ever had in his life. The new creation had arrived.

Adapting
". . . God changed . . ."—Exodus 32:14

The most difficult struggle with starting any medication is continuing to take it. During the first few days, the medicated often experience a wide variety of substantial side effects. Imagine your stomach feeling like you were just punched in the gut. Consider what it be like to feel drowsiness that lasts for days. Think about a medication that makes you crazier before it makes you better. The body just takes time to adjust to anything new in the system. Ponder having to continue taking the medication in the midst of all of these side effects and more. Then, consider that sometimes these side effects last for an extended period of time. While the intensity of the side effects are different from person to person and from medication to medication, there is no medication that doesn't have a period of adjustment.

Some call it medication. Some call it poison. In that adjustment period, God most certainly would've called it poison. God's stomach felt like it was being ripped to shreds. God kept having trouble waking up. God felt crazier than ever before. Even though God struggled to believe it, God kept reminding the divine mind that the side effects wouldn't last forever.

The medicine was about love. When God created humanity, God was looking for love. Forced love is not love. Careful not to force anything, God created and took the pill of humanity. The problem is that God didn't know what to do with the creatures. Staying distant, God put humanity in the Garden of Eden " . . . to till it and keep it." (Genesis 2:15). Basically, God wanted to keep humanity busy until God could figure out what to do with them. The side effects were excruciating. God had never wanted to talk to anyone before. God had never felt the need to take care of anyone before. God had always lived with little responsibility. God didn't like being this close to anything. The human medication was very difficult. God grew crazier with every interaction.

"Please just take the medicine!" I'd been off of my medication for a little while. Things did not turn out so good. Those who loved me pushed me to go to the psychiatrist. The psychiatrist pushed me to go back on the medication. Despite warnings that going back on would be a difficult adjustment, I started taking my medication again. The side effects were excruciating. I needed space from everything. I felt so burdened with a wide variety of responsibilities. I felt out of my mind. My psychiatrist told me that such an extreme reaction is the first sign that the medication is actually working.

Medications keep on creating. The more you take the pills the more you change. While it's impossible to tell whether the change will be good or bad, one can only hope that adhering to a prescription will make one feel better. Initially, God thought that one dose would do the trick. God was wrong. Mental illness is usually not subdued with one treatment. One must be vigilant in treatment. God needed to keep taking the medication. Every pill brought something new. Creation continued. " . . . It is not good for humanity to be alone . . ." (Genesis 2:18). Before God knew it, there were tons of people in the Garden of Eden. Every pill seemed to bring a new batch. While God knew that it was " . . . not good for humanity to be alone . . ." (2:18), God also knew that all of the newness was taking God to the limit. Creation made God crazy. The medication didn't seem to be helping with all of the anxiety that kept rushing in. When God engaged with the humans, God couldn't figure out what was real. Everything seemed to be a hallucination. Maybe it was? What difference would it make? Who's to say what is real and what is false? Sometimes you have to engage with the hallucinations just to survive.

Some people are zealous to get on medication, not Nikki. "I've never understood those people." Throughout her treatment, Nikki resisted the doctor's efforts to medicate her. "I have no interest in being changed." Change was something she hated. Before knowing that she was mentally ill, society told her that she was wrong and sinful based on who she was. "I'm not interested in what society has to say." One night, things went to shit and Nikki ended up in a jail cell. Grabbing her head, Nikki decided that it was time to take the doctor's advice. When she got out the next morning, she knew where she was headed. "I'm here to take your advice." Not long after starting the medication, Nikki began changing. "No one realizes how much you adjust to mental illness." Every pill brought something new. Nikki didn't like it. The change was too much. Before Nikki knew it, there was change everywhere. The change made Nikki feel so alone. "It is not good for Nikki to be alone." Creation made her crazier. Unable to figure out what was real, Nikki isolated her self until the adjusting was over. The visions didn't leave. "Who are you?" Sometimes you have to engage the hallucinations. "What are you?" In time, the experience of creating a new Nikki became the most real experience she ever had.

Though difficult and unpredictable, adjusting to medication is always successful at making the treated feel one thing . . . alive. Whether the side effects or adjustments are good or bad, the treated feels something. The process of feeling your way to a better space is what treatment is all about. During this time, you learn to grow and feel " . . . not ashamed." (Genesis 2:25). While there are certainly highs and lows, treatment is about becoming a new creation. In treatment, God was becoming something different. The old creation was becoming a new creation.

Fall
" . . . the serpent was more crafty . . ."—Genesis 3:1

In the darkness, God couldn't find the pills. Growing angrier by the second, God cursed the darkness and demanded light. The light wouldn't listen and the darkness grew. Unsure of what was happening, God searched for the humans. Looking through dimensions and space, God realized that someone stole the medicine. When the humans acted evil, God lashed out in rage. Unable to control the divine emotions, God started swinging. Before you know it, God lashed out at the humans and destroyed Eden. When God finally found the medication hidden near God, God blamed the other God in the divine mind. Once the medication kicked in, God couldn't believe what God had done.

Adjustment

"What is this that you have done?"—Genesis 3:13

THROUGHOUT HIS LIFE, CHARLES struggled with fits of rage. During a particularly disturbing incident, Charles savagely beat a cat to death. "What have I done?" Psychologists simply assumed that Charles would grow out of it. At school, Charles was an incredible guy. Everyone wanted to be around him. One day after he got into a particularly brutal fight, one of Charles' teachers realized that he needed professional help. Eventually, Charles got on medication that helped to control his rage. For many years, Charles did fine. Then, the world grew dark. Bad things kept happening to Charles and he decided to stop taking his medication. Driving home one day, Charles became enraged at a slow older driver and rammed her car. If something hadn't clicked, Charles would've killed her. Everything stopped when Charles heard the voice of his mother saying, "What is this you have done?" (Genesis 3:13). When Charles got back on medication he couldn't believe what happened.

Adjustments bring moments of disbelief. There is an inability to comprehend what is going on. The mind is suspended in a state of malfunction. God knows the feeling. God was there. The medication created all sorts of new creation. Eden was the most beautiful of them all. Instead of finding compassion and grace in the midst of darkness, God destroyed the light. You can't blame it on God. Without medication, God didn't know any better. God was still adjusting. Adjustments are always more severe when you are going on and off the medication. Looking down at Eden, the question kept rolling around in God's mind "What is this that you have done?" (Genesis 3:13). The destruction of Eden was catastrophic. As the adjustment extended, there would be more catastrophes. The question would continue to roll around. "What is this you have done?" The object of the question would only get worse.

Rage
". . . God sent them out . . ."—Genesis 3:23

Though the initial adjustment was far more difficult than God ever anticipated, God loved humanity and humanity loved God. For the first time, God was able to combat divine loneliness with real conversation. The more God talked the more God found love. Conversation draws people in deeper. God knew what it was like to be alone. For eternity, God talked to the voices shouting in the divine mind. Humanity was capable of love. Humanity was capable of conversation with real consequence. God made sure of it. God didn't want a new creation that was easily controlled. Humanity was never easily controlled. Medication is never easily controlled. There are always unintended consequences.

Love is never without it's consequences. The relationship between humanity and God grew. The potential for great pain also grew. God was not prepared to be hurt. The consequences were devastating. God couldn't control the divine thoughts. One of the consequences of the new medication was a war in the divine mind. The voices kept telling God to run away from the humans. "If you don't destroy them they will destroy you." God was terrified of love. Anxiety kept metastasizing throughout the body. The entire heavenly realm was shaking. God had to get rid of the humans. God had to get off the medication. In a fit of rage, God planted the tree in Eden. Knowing that the knowledge of good and evil would be too attractive to resist, God planted that damn tree right in the middle of the humans. God thought this would provide a good reason to destroy humanity. Ultimately, the tree was disturbed and the deed was done. While humanity was responsible for the deed, the deed wouldn't have been possible if God hadn't put the tree there in the first place. Is the one who disobeyed God crazier than the God who facilitated the disobedience? Regardless, the rage of God only grew. God was ready to destroy everything. Then it happened. Love knocked the shit out of God. For a moment, God was able to let all humans out of Eden without succumbing to the rage that was gnawing at the divine mind.

"Stop! Please! We love you!" Sierra was really off the rails this time. Screaming about murdering and killing, Sierra walked from room to room. Nobody knew what to do. The condition seemed to be getting worse. Late one afternoon, Sierra got a hold of a gun. Enraged, Sierra ran around and pointed the gun at her family. "I'm going to handle all of these humans once and for all!" The rage grew. Then it happened. Sierra saw her mother and calmed down long enough for everyone to get out. Nobody thought twice about running out the door except for Sierra's mother. With the police at the door, Sierra was terrified. Eventually, Sierra's mother talked long enough to get her to put the gun down. Paramedics took her to a hospital. The rage subsided. Love was enough to save a few lives.

Depression

" . . . on that day all the fountains of the great deep burst forth, and the windows of the heavens were opened. The rain fell on the earth forty days and forty nights."—Genesis 7:11-12

God didn't understand what was going on. Tears flowed faster and faster. Sadness created more sadness. Darkness was everywhere and closing in. When the darkness finally darkened everything that was and was to be, God collapsed into an explosion of hopelessness. "How do I make it stop?" Looking to the humans, God decided that more humans would only make everything worse. "I thought you were supposed to help me!" Unable to move, God stayed in bed. Unable to speak, God gave up on words. Unable to even think, God only knew despair. The tears were God's only companions. God made so many of them. The only thing the depression accomplished was pain. The world quickly filled with tears.

While God initially created water to cleanse, God's tears destroyed. God didn't care. God was ready for everything to end. With water flowing from every direction, the earth started to fill. Thinking about the consequences of destroying everything, God decided that there was a need to save part of the medication. Noah and his family were encouraged to build an Ark. The tears kept flowing. God hoped to drown God in the process. The screams and cries of the drowning never hit God's ears. The depression was too powerful. Water continued to rise. God didn't care. God was too engulfed in God's own pain. God didn't care about Noah either. God just wanted to drown. When the darkness finally lifted, God waited for eternity before God looked to see what happened. Scared of what might be, God checked on Noah first. Noah and his family were ok. Afraid of triggering God's depression again, no one dared to tell God what God did. Though God couldn't help it, the devastation was great. "I flooded everything!" Devastated at the consequences of this side effect, God pursued further adjustment.

Throughout his life, Abala suffered from terrible bouts of depression. While the manifestations were different, the result was always the same. Tears flowed faster and faster. Sadness birthed more sadness. Choking darkness closed in. Hopelessness smothered the future. Depression took everything. When Abala started the new medication, he thought everything would get better. Abala had no idea he would have to go through the worst depression he'd ever faced to get there. The floodgates opened. Eventually, Abala lost his family. No one wanted to deal with this level of depression. The tears rose until they drowned everything in his life. Water was supposed to cleanse. Water was all that Abala knew. Abala couldn't breathe. When the waters eventually subsided, Abala was alone. "How could tears cause such destruction?" Realizing that he had to do something different, Abala searched for an adjustment.

Questions

"*. . . you anoint my head . . ."*—Psalm 23:5

Trees blurred by my window. Life seemed to blur with every second. The road moved back and forth. Nothing was the same. The suicide changed all of our lives. Walking up to the big white church, I didn't want to go in. I felt numb. God had already failed enough. I wasn't interested in giving God the opportunity to fail again. The big doors opened. Though I talked to people, I don't remember it. We made it to our seats on the reserved second row. In the midst of suicide, the pastor chose to read Psalm 23. The narcissism of God was on full display. Questions about a God who would want us to find comfort in such words were too.

> God is my shepherd,
>
> *So this is about you?*
>
> I shall not want.
>
> *I shall not want my uncle to be alive?*
>
> God makes me lie down in green pastures;
>
> *Where?*
>
> God leads me beside still waters;
>
> *When?*
>
> God restores my soul.
>
> *Today?*
>
> God leads me in right paths;
>
> *Is a right path to be sitting here mourning my uncle?*
>
> For God's name's sake.
>
> *So this is about you?*
>
> Even though I walk
>
> *How am I supposed to even move?*
>
> Through the darkest valley,
>
> *Why am I even here?*

I will fear no evil;

Are you the greatest threat?

For you are with me;

Why haven't you done anything?

Your rod and you staff -

Is this a joke?

They comfort me.

Does everything have to be about you?

You prepare a table before me

Do you not realize that your record on preparation is rough?

In the presence of my enemies;

Why haven't you sat down with your enemies?

You anoint my head with oil;

When was the last time you got your head examined?

My cup overflows.

Who actually believes this shit?

Surely goodness and mercy will follow me

Is this goodness and mercy following me?

All the days of my life,

Will you take care of me like you did my uncle?

And I shall dwell in the house of God forever.

Is this the consequence of dwelling in your house?

Before the beginning, God struggled with narcissism. After the beginning, God struggled with narcissism. Before the end, God will struggle with narcissism. After the end, God will struggle with narcissism. Eternally, God struggles with narcissism. How else do you explain God creating entire worlds to praise God?

Sex Addiction
"Your two breasts are like two fawns, twins of a gazelle . . ."
-Song of Solomon 4:5

The glow moved across the face of God. The breasts danced. The dick pulsated. The tongue licked. The vagina moistened. The orgasm exploded. There were also always surprises too. From encounter to climax, every second drew God in. Unable to turn away, God watched and masturbated. Every orgasm brought the immediate yearning for another. God knew that God had a problem. God was addicted to sex.

The humans were making God worse. One of the powerful side effects of the medication was that God was aroused all the time. There had to be a way to stop this. Masturbating was the only thing that helped. While certainly not what the writer intended it to be, the Song of Solomon eventually turned into God's favorite pornography. God loved the language. God loved the fawn breasts. God loved the thrusting. God loved the huge penis. God loved the imagery. God loved the moistness. God loved the dirty sex. God loved it all. The Song of Solomon always left God wanting more. The scenes played out in the mind of God eternally. Humans tortured God. The orgasms were just not intense or frequent enough. God just kept doing the same thing over and over expecting a different result.

Living alone in an urban apartment, John had no friends. Truthfully, John didn't need any friends. There was only one thing that John needed . . . sex. While most would prefer to have sex with another, John preferred to have sex with himself. From the comfort of his bedroom, John could get lost in the images and have as many orgasms as he wanted. For years, John spent every waking moment pursuing the next orgasm. When he was fired from his job for looking at pornography at work, John realized that he had a problem. John sought the advice of his pastor. The pastor tried to secure as much information as possible about the images. John felt like his pastor was getting too distracted by the content to be of any help. Eventually, John went to see a psychologist. The office was warm and inviting. After some conversation, the psychologist didn't hesitate to tell John the truth, "You're a sex addict. You need to go to rehab." John knew this was the right path. "You can't heal on your own." When John left for rehab, he knew that God was with him.

Bones

". . . set me down in the middle of a valley; it was full of bones . . ."— *Ezekiel 37:1*

Sicknesses of the mind ravage the body down to the bone. "I never thought I would eat so much." "I never thought I would attempt suicide." "I never thought I would do drugs." "I never thought I would stop exercising." "I never thought I would be so violent." "I never thought . . ." The troubled mind drags the sufferer to places they never thought they would go. God knows that place. Ezekiel did too. Life is quickly extinguished there. Bones are all that is left. The valley continues to fill.

For many years, West hid her secret. Every night, West ate until she couldn't eat anymore. When she finished, West purged everything. Since West never gained weight, nobody could tell that West suffered from a food obsession. Eventually, medical problems made West stop purging. Unable to stop eating, West ballooned in weight. Unable to face her new reality, West quit her job. Unable to leave the house due to her size, West started to lose her life. The process only seemed to speed up. West never thought she would feel like there was nothing more to her than bones. Realizing she needed help, West started to consider treatment. The pull of the food filled her mind. "I just need to breathe!"

God couldn't breathe. The anxiety was too much. Humanity wanted more and more. God couldn't meet the demand. Sweat poured. The stomach growled. What was God going to do? "These creatures were supposed to help!" Running into things, God desperately reached for the medication. The problem was that the medication always brought new creation and God was terrified. Unable to stomach the medication, God collapsed. The anxiety had God on the floor. God felt like life was fleeting. God felt like death was certain. God felt like a pile of bones. Every breath was more difficult than the last. God couldn't keep on doing this. "I just need to breathe!"

"Can these bones live?" Ezekiel stood with God pondering the question. After a moment, Ezekiel looked up to God and said, " . . . you know." (Ezekiel 37:3). Was God talking about the divine bones? Was God talking about the bones strewn throughout the valley? What's the difference? In the midst of this wild scene of bones, God gave Ezekiel instructions about life. " . . . Prophesy to the breath . . ." (37:9). Life requires more than bones. Bones cannot move without breath. The bones started to shake. For the first time, God realized that God needed further treatment. While the bones moved, God tried to figure out the next move. "How do I breathe?" God grew afraid. The anxiety spiked. The sweat returned. The fear won. Knowing that God needed needed further treatment, God ran.

Running
"Go at once to Ninevah . . ."—Jonah 1:2

God is with us. God is in us. God goes beside us. God goes before us. God goes. The story of Jonah is the story of a God that is not still. Jonah was made in the image of God. In short, God goes wherever Jonah does. When Jonah gets to running away from Nineveh, God runs too. God is just as disobedient as Jonah. There is nothing that Jonah does that God isn't present for. Jonah takes God with him. There is also a part of God that doesn't go. The story of Jonah is about competing the personalities of God. The many personalities of God combine to put tremendous pressure on the divine mind. The voices kept screaming. The commands keep conflicting. The personalities bring chaos. The psychosis only worsens. The story of Jonah is the story of the struggle to control the divine mind in the midst of mental illness. Nineveh was supposed to make God better. Nineveh was supposed to lead to the next treatment. One part of God demanded that Jonah go to Nineveh. Unfortunately, the other part of God refused to go and took off with Jonah. God fighting God led to a whale of a tale.

"What is this that you have done!" (Jonah 1:10). In the midst of the running, Jonah ended up on a boat. God was in the middle of a melt down. The winds blew. The lightening crashed. The thunder shook the world. God's personalities wanted to go separate ways. The entire world suffered the consequences of God's psychosis. Everyone was given over to fear. Jonah was terrified. God and Jonah thought they could save everyone if they just jumped in the water. This was the closest that either God or Jonah had ever come to suicide. Unable to go through with it, Jonah and God asked to be thrown into the water. The sailors obliged. Instead of drowning, the two were swallowed by a large fish. Unable to separate thoughts and voices, God wasn't sure who sent the fish. Nevertheless, the chaos in the mind of God created a truly disgusting situation. In the darkness of the belly of the large fish, God wrestled with the voices. Resisting Nineveh, God still thought God could handle all of it on God's own. Jonah just prayed. Unfortunately, the many divine personalities made it difficult to know which manifestation of God Jonah was actually praying to. When God decided that it was time for further treatment, the large fish spewed both God and Jonah onto dry land. Having second thoughts, God changed the divine mind on Nineveh. Looking at God's self, God screamed, "I don't need no damn treatment! I'm fine!"

"Get up, go to Nineveh . . ." (Jonah 3:2). Jonah and God had to go to the place that God told them to go to in the first place. God's mind struggled back and forth the entire journey. "I don't want to go!" Fear obstructed every step. When they finally arrived for treatment, the people greeted them warmly. Begging for grace, the people implored God, "Please seek treatment!" For a second, God was going to embrace the treatment offered in the city. Then, Jonah and God changed their mind. After forgiving the people for even trying, God left quickly. Up on a hill overlooking the city, God wrestled with God. Jonah just got knocked around. The mind of God was exploding with noises, urges, sounds and voices. "It is better for me to die than to live" (4:8). Near annihilation, God slowly died.

Death

" . . . the day of death is better than the day of birth."—Ecclesiastes 7:1

"I can't wait to die." The words startled everyone. Mary was just being honest. For many years, Mary suffered from a disease of the mind that left her depressed and angry all the time. "Who wouldn't look forward to death if they had to live like I do?" Something within Mary refused to let her give up. With the help of friends, Mary checked into a treatment center. Doctors promised a rebirth. You will feel totally new after this treatment. Strapped to a gurney, the doctors rolled Mary down the hallway. The terror hit when Mary saw the sign over the door, "Shock Therapy." Now Mary knew for sure, " . . . the day of death is better than the day of birth."

"I don't think I can fight anymore." God was talking to God again. On occasion, the personalities stopped fighting long enough to talk civilly. Psychosis accompanied the stench of death. God knew that God kept fucking up. Repeatedly, God killed people for no reason. God didn't want God's condition to keep destroying life. "I'm ready to pull the plug on everything." Due to the eternal psychosis, God knew that the day of God's death would be so much better that the day of God's birth. Death was so tempting. Annihilation sounded like bliss. The final questions rolled around the divine mind. Though there were many attractive lethal answers, God couldn't just end it all. With so much riding on the decision, God wasn't ready to give up yet. Something within God pushed God toward treatment. "I just need help." The mania grew wilder. The depression became more blinding. The voices drowned everything out. The anxiety was crippling. The mind exploded and contracted repeatedly. God was dealing with everything. Desperate, God decided to fully embrace the medicine. When God arrived, God was strapped to a gurney and rolled down the hallway. God willed it all. The divine mind needed the strongest dose possible. Going to the back, God saw the sign, "Earth" and started to resist. The personalities of God fought so hard that God kept rolling forward. Before God dropped to humanity, God prayed that the shock therapy of becoming human would be exactly what would help the divine mind. Falling into a stable full of shit, God screamed out in pain.

Shock

"In the beginning was the Shock, the Shock was with God and the Shock was God."-John 1:1

DOCTORS ORDERED GOD INSTITUTIONALIZED. The shock of incarnation was what they prescribed. Connectors were placed on God's head. The gurney rolled forward. God wrestled back and forth. The fight was real. God didn't know if God could handle being amongst humans. The emotions required were too intense. God didn't want to be one of them. There was tremendous power in being God alone. God was the eternal shock. How could these humans ever shock God? Though the divine thoughts raced, God was strapped in and slowly rolling toward the door. There was no turning back. God already signed all the forms. The psychosis was out of control. God needed big help. The doors swung open. Sweat dropped off of God's forehead. "NO!!!" God screamed. Light flooded. The institutionalization of the incarnation felt like falling. Landing with a thud, God cried out at the first shock. The smell of stable shit in Bethlehem was unlike anything God had encountered before. God's incarnational institutionalization would bring about many more shocks.

Blood splattered on the walls. Broken glass littered the floor. Life flowed out of dozens of bodies. Survivors screamed out in pain. The shooter surrendered. For the next few days, Whitney kept repeatedly screaming strange things. Psychologists and psychiatrists determined that Whitney was mentally ill. The judge declared that Whitney would spend the rest of her life in treatment for mental illness. After rushing the judge, Whitney had to be tackled by deputies, placed on a gurney and taken to the state mental hospital. For months, doctors studied Whitney crashing and spinning her way around a padded room. After numerous medications failed, doctors realized that they only had one more option. It took more than 10 people to get Whitney strapped to the gurney. Even as they rolled her down the hallway, Whitney screamed and managed to break the wrist strap. Workers quickly replaced the strap and kept pushing. Doctors placed the connectors on Whitney's head. The first shock was unlike anything Whitney had ever felt before. As her entire body seized, Whitney closed her eyes and let the electricity flow through her body. The anesthesia finally took over from there. As Whitney started to show signs of improvement, doctors repeated the procedure. For years, doctors shocked Whitney's brain. Over time, Whitney improved. One morning before treatment, Whitney told her doctor, "I feel like I've been reborn."

No one goes to a mental institution for fun. Trauma is always involved. For many, they are dealing with deadly sicknesses that could easily kill unless they get help soon. God was so sick by the end of the Old Testament. God killed so many people. Bodies and blood littered the floor. Trauma overtook God's life. Afraid that God might continue killing, God was institutionalized in the incarnation. Just being institutionalized wasn't enough. God needed serious treatment. Shock therapy is a treatment of last resort. No one chooses shock therapy. Only the sickest are forced to get shock therapy. God was the sickest.

Addiction
"When the wine gave out . . ."—John 2:3

God wrestled with God. God wanted to quit forever. God needed more. God tried to stop. God couldn't stop. God was addicted.

Phillip loved going to weddings. While everyone engaged in the ceremony, Phillip always went to the back and got a few drinks in. Phillip loved drinking more than anything else in life. After his wife and kids left him and he got sick, wine was the only thing

Phillip had to live for. When he was invited to a friend's wedding in Cana of Galilee, Phillip was excited. These folks were very wealthy and would be able to provide as much sweet wine as he could drink. On the day of the wedding, Phillip was drunk before he ever arrived. Drinking was his only practice. Right after Phillip woke up that morning, he drank wine. Throughout the day, Phillip drank wine. Right before arriving to the ceremony, Phillip drank wine. Sneaking out back, Phillip found the wine. Sure enough, the taste was as sweet as any wine he'd ever had and he could drink all that he wanted. Phillip drank and drank. The wine started to give out.

"This is unbelievable!" God was amazed. Everyone was so happy. God had never been to a wedding before. From the moment God walked in, all God felt was love. The couple seemed to fall more in love by the second. The families were so proud. Everyone was there in the moment as if nothing else was going on in any other part of the world. When the band kicked off and the food was served, the wine started to flow. "I need a couple of glasses." Wine was God's favorite thing since being institutionalized. For hours, God drank and drank. Everyone was drunk. When the wine started to give out, God turned six water jars into wine. "Where did this wine come from?" Nobody could figure out where the wine came from. Then, nobody seemed to care. People just kept drinking. After God felt the shock of being drunk for the first time, God met Phillip. The wine kept flowing. Like they were long lost friends, God and Phillip danced to the band, spilled wine on the floor and hung on each other for long periods of time. While sitting on the floor drunk, God had an out of body experience. Looking at both God and Phillip lying on the floor drunk, God realized that neither one of them could stop drinking even if they wanted to. They were alcoholics. Though terrifying, God kept drinking to chase away the pain. Every swallow made God feel better until God got sick. Out amongst the flowers, God started throwing up. Phillip tried to make sure that God was ok. Then, Phillip threw up. For some time, God and Phillip threw up together. With chunks of dinner littering their clothes, God and Phillip laid on the ground waiting for help. The disciples finally arrived and helped get both

of them home. The next morning the disciples had an intervention with God. Realizing that he couldn't leave Phillip, God had
an intervention with him too. Thinking back to all the times that
God couldn't stop drinking, God was shocked by how completely
substances can take over the brain. God had no idea that God carried an addicted brain.

Mania

"Making a whip of cords, God drove all of them out of the temple . . ."
—John 2:15

Traveling always did a number on Maria's brain. The new medicine
was making things worse. "Why am I being so aggressive?" The
question was rhetorical. Maria knew the answer. Mania was setting
in. Thought she hated the feeling and knew that she was dangerous
while manic, Maria was afraid of what would happen if she stopped
taking the medicine. Far from doctors or mental healthcare, Maria
simply had to push through. Maria prayed for help. While she was
walking down a cobblestone street, a motorcyclist hit Maria and
broke her watch. When the motorcyclist stopped to see if she was
ok, the mania exploded. Maria took a large rock and started to destroy the motorcycle. No one could stop her. Bystanders had never
seen rage like this before. After the motorcycle was rendered inoper-
able, Maria walked away feeling justified. Everyone just got out of
the way. Many days later, Maria couldn't believe what she'd done.

God never liked going to the Temple. Passover was an especially rough time. The leaders saw these days as a prime opportunity to make money. Due to their lack of resources, many people
who wanted to worship were turned away. God was disgusted by
the injustice of it all. Throughout the week, God kept his rage in
check. Then, things changed. When they walked into the Temple,
the disciples could see a noticeable change in God's mood. The
leaders of the Temple kept committing injustices by ripping people
off and refusing them access to the Temple. God couldn't take it
anymore. The mania of God exploded. Screaming out, God started
swinging around a whip that God made. Cracking the whip over

and over, God destroyed the tools of injustice. The oppressors ran out screaming. God destroyed all of their products. When people complained, God responded with rapid conversation. God was even ready to rebuild and destroy the Temple in three days. With mania like God was experiencing, anything was possible.

Hallucinations
". . . tempted by the devil."—Luke 4:2

The devil was in the mind of God. How could such evil terrorize God from within? God couldn't figure it out. God just kept wrestling. The temptations were so strong. God felt like God was consistently being transported to different places. The mind of God was so confused. The devil was a part of God. Was this an internal or external threat? God demanded answers. The problem was that God couldn't think. Divine hallucinations are so strong.

"The devil lives in my ear!" Martha screamed at the doctor. For over an hour, the doctor kept asking her what was wrong. The answer was always the same. "The devil lives in my ear!" The doctor refused to engage such foolishness. Prescribing her more and more medication, the doctor tried to get the paranoia and hallucinations under control. Nothing seemed to work. Martha was most terrified when the lights went out. Throughout the night, the devil talked to her from the foot of her bed. Tempting her with all sorts of foolishness, the devil consistently taunted and abused Martha. When the morning came, the devil would go back in her ear until the next night. Realizing that medication wasn't working, the doctor called the chaplain. "I need an exorcism!" After some conversation and planning, the chaplain obliged. When the exorcism began, Martha struggled violently against every word. The doctor said that such struggles were common with patients enduring intense hallucinations. The chaplain encouraged Martha to fight back against the devil. "Get out of my ear!" Martha kept talking to the devil. The doctor said that patients engage the hallucinations like they would in real life. "It is finished." Then, Martha collapsed. The doctor said that it was common for patients to collapse after extreme hallucinations. Martha woke up normal. "I'm ready to begin my earthly ministry." The doctor was ecstatic. "I've finally cured Martha with the right combination of medicine!"

God's brain was acting up. The disciples kept asking God if God was ok. "I'm not going to do it!" God kept screaming out in confusion. God tried to get advice from multiple healers. No one knew what to do. The disciples grew more and more fearful. Nobody knew what to do. "I can't!" "Please!" "I won't!" "Stop!" God screamed out in pain. The voices kept pummeling the mind of God. "I keep seeing things." God knew that everything was getting worse. In fear, God fled to the wilderness. For forty days, God struggled with the devil. Throughout the experience, God didn't know if the devil was in front of God or a product of the mind of God. The hallucinations were as real as anything God ever experienced. The temptation to commit suicide or annihilation was something that God experienced eternally. When it was all over, God felt cured. What happened? God didn't know. The only thing that God knew was that it wasn't over. God was shocked that the brain could harbor such powerful hallucinations.

Narcissism

"... I am the light of the world."—John 8:12

John was selfish. Everyday, the only thing that John cared to think about was John. People were amazed at how much time John invested in John. While at home, all John wanted to do was watch old videos of John. For hours, John would stand in front to of the mirror to perfect his appearance. While at work, John consistently reminded everyone that John was the greatest employee the company ever hired. After work, John went to the gym and watched John work out in the mirrors. At night, John never had sex with anyone because he only liked to masturbate to his own image. To say that no one liked John was an understatement. Only John liked John and John could never understand why.

There was an injustice that was about to take place. The narcissistic Pharisees caught a woman committing adultery and were going to kill her. God stepped in and saved her life. Instead of walking away with her to make sure that she was ok, God stood up and proclaimed, "I am the light of the world." The interaction was a battle of narcissists. The Pharisees wanted to display their power and God wanted to display God's power. This was not the first time that God made such a statement. Throughout the institutionaliza-tion of the incarnation, God consistently talked about God in the most glowing terms imaginable. When one of the disciples pulled God aside, God was shocked to realize that even God had propen-sities toward narcissism.

Depression
". . . I am deeply grieved, even to death . . ."—Mark 14:34

Sarah tried to have a child. Throughout her wait, Sarah experi-enced a prolonged depression. Unable to shake the misery, Sarah lost her mind. Lying in bed, Sarah couldn't remember important facts. When the numbness hit, Sarah was grateful. Darkness was all that Sarah knew. Eventually, Sarah got pregnant. For a time, Sarah was very happy. Then, tragedy hit. Sarah lost the baby. Depression hit Sarah worse than she'd ever experienced. Feeling like someone was standing on her heart, Sarah started to cut her wrists. Feeling grieved unto death, Sarah bled.

The blackout curtains were pulled tight. Darkness flooded every corner of the room. Mario hadn't been out of his bedroom in weeks. "God has abandoned me." Unable to shake his sense that God was gone, Mario loudly prayed day and night. "Answer me!" Mario only knew the excruciating pain of abandonment. There were no answers. There were only requests. Mario kept going to his knees. The depression only seemed to grow. "Why is God torturing me?" When Mario's employer called to tell him he was fired, Mario shrugged. God was the only thing that mattered. Now, God was gone. Mario prayed so much that his knees bled. "Why?" Unable to understand his suffering, Mario vowed not to leave the room until he got word from God. The darkness only seemed to intensify.

God knew there were people after God. Rumors of crucifixion filled the air. God knew that there was real reason to be fearful. The problem was that God seemed destined to walk right into it. God developed this idea that God had to die. The only thing that God knew was what God told God. God told God that God had to die. While God questioned God, God felt like God had to follow what God said. God's mind was made up. Hours before God knew that God's enemies were coming, God went to the Garden of Gethsemane to pray. The disciples were unable to understand the level of depression that God was experiencing. Especially grieved and agitated, God struggled to even function. Begging the disciples to stand with God, God went deeper into the Garden alone. Screaming out to God, God begged for the shock to stop. "Stop!" God just got one jolt after the other. The depression fought back. God was getting worse. God grew weaker and weaker. The depression was crushing God. When God realized the disciples were all asleep, God felt the strongest jolt yet. The depression was so bad that God started to feel a physical pain unlike anything that God had ever experienced. The shock hit again and blood started to pour from the pores of God. Depression won. God fully felt the embodied weight of every mental illness to ever exist. Electricity overcame everything and God was taken away.

Results
"It is God!"—John 21:7

The only way to bring God through the most severe characteristics of mental illness was to take God there. God embodied mental illness in the flesh. Every shock of embodied mental illness revealed to God a more divine way of being God. Embodied addiction helped God to understand divine sobriety. Embodied mania helped God better understand divine instances of chaos. Embodied hallucinations helped God better understand divine psychosis. Embodied narcissism helped God better understand uncontrollable divine arrogance. Embodied depression helped God better understand divine helplessness. The incarnation was about a struggle for control of the divine mind in the midst of mental illness. Ultimately, God knew that God was going to be crucified. God was so exhausted by God's various mental illnesses that God chose to die. God died. This was the most divine interaction with mental illness that has ever existed. God thought that the mental illness would die if God died. Mental illness survived death. Psychosis is eternal. The last shock was when God realized that mental illness was a part of who God eternally is. The institutionalization that was the incarnation shocked God into a place of knowing how to live with mental illness. The liberation of a mentally ill God is found in God's realization that mental illness is divine. Our liberation is too.

Stay

"While staying with them . . ."—Acts 1:4

SHOCK THERAPY FINALLY HAD Pooja's depression under control. Even though she was feeling much better, doctors advised her to stay in the hospital for a few days to keep track of the side effects. For a time, there were no side effects. Then, they hit. First, Pooja experienced disorientation. Unable to figure out what was where, Pooja had to call for help multiple times. Second, Pooja was loose headed. On two different occasions, Pooja was unable to stand and fell. Third, Pooja experienced hallucinations. Looking out the window, Pooja thought she saw all sorts of creatures coming into her room. Ultimately, she screamed. Though she was definitely improving, the stay was difficult.

God never left. Though the shock therapy helped tremendously, mental illness is never healed. God stayed amongst the people seeking wider wellness. The institutionalization of the incarnation continued. God was prepared for the side effects. There would be a few.

Crazy

". . . suddenly from heaven there came a sound like the rush of a violent wind . . ."—Acts 2:2

God was disoriented. Shock therapy is not for the faint of heart. Stumbling around the room, God kept blowing as hard as God could. The blowing turned into a wind. God didn't stop. For some reason, God thought blowing would make the disorientation go away. Then, God tried to start a fire. After a few attempts, God was successful. Picking up the hot coals, God started flinging fire everywhere. Then, God made all the humans speak different yet understandable languages. God grew more disoriented and kept manipulating the humans in the midst of God's disorientation. Finally, God was able to gain some control over the divine mind. Knowing that the disorientation was a side effect of the shock therapy, God tried not to worry about it. Looking up, God couldn't believe that Peter was trying to spin God's disorientation as a religious experience. Pentecost was a side effect of treatment for God's mental illness.

Fahad stumbled around the block. People couldn't understand what was going on. Thinking he was somewhere else, Fahad kept screaming about incomprehensible things. Frequent disorientation was a part of Fahad's mental condition. The visions grew more and more intense. Fahad thought that he was having a religious experience. Everyone else thought that Fahad belonged in a mental institution. When Fahad was able to get control of his mind, Fahad agreed with them. In time, Fahad got worse. Ultimately, Fahad decided to go talk to his religious leader about being institutionalized for a time. The religious leader tried to convince Fahad that he was having a religious experience when the disorientation hit. Knowing better, Fahad decided to find a new religious leader.

God knew that God was under attack. God sent wind against God's enemies. When that didn't work, God sent tongues of fire. The wind and tongues of fire combined to create quite the scene. The enemies of God acted crazier than ever. Terrified, God divided their language to confuse them. The language division didn't work. The people seemed to somehow understand what each other was saying. God felt like they might be greater than God. The fear deepened. God was afraid of a takeover. Paranoia spun like a mighty wind. Then, God collapsed. Once God came out of the haze, God realized that the enemies were actually followers of God. In the midst of the confusion, God had a temporary break with reality that lead to Pentecost.

Love

"... the greatest of these is love."— *1 Corinthians 13:13*

God's mind was fucked. Extreme thought killed every normal thought. God couldn't even breathe right. Divine war raged. God's heart exploded. The relapse into psychosis was the worst that God had experienced yet. God couldn't get control of God's brain. Crazy was all God knew. God heard the tongues of humans trying to speak to God. This sounded like a noisy gong being beat repeatedly in the divine mind. All God heard was bang after bang. God's brain spiraled further. Angels tried to help God. This sounded like a clanging cymbal right next to the divine ear. All God heard was tink tink tink. God couldn't figure out what was going on. In the midst of the deep psychosis, God reached for all mysteries and knowledge to help. All God found was deeper confusion. There were no answers to the craziness. God reached for a divine faith that could normally accomplish anything. God's faith failed. A mountain fell on God's face. God felt like God was nothing. The depression grew. God tried to do something with the divine body. The divine mind only continued to crash. Brain explosions took away everything. God was a child. God spoke like a child. God was desperate for some help. God couldn't even see straight. Everything seemed like a dim mirror. Nothing was clear. God's mind was fucked. Though hesitant, God took the strongest dose of love that God could find. God regained something eternal.

Extreme thoughts rushed her eyes. Melissa couldn't figure out what was real. Was that a person with big teeth or a deadly animal? Oxygen was hard to come by. Paranoia flooded every crevice of Melissa's body. Fighting anyone who came near, Melissa let it be known that she didn't need any help. The world spiraled into a wild fucking abyss. Relapse couldn't even begin to describe the battle that Melissa was facing. The brain was out of control. Melissa couldn't catch it. Crazy birthed crazy. Melissa heard the terrifying tongues of humans. Fearful of what was going to happen next, Melissa ran. Looking into the clouds, Melissa thought she saw angels. Repeatedly, Melissa heard the sounds of noisy gongs and clanging cymbals. There was an out of control parade of chaos going on in Melissa's brain and she wasn't invited. Mysteries and knowledge flowed through the sky. Jumping around, Melissa failed at grabbing them. Confusion buried Melissa alive. There were no answers. Faith felt like oppression. A mountain fell on Melissa's head. Melissa was functioning on the level of a child. Melissa couldn't understand anything. There seemed to be no brain left. Melissa couldn't see straight. Everything seemed to be blacked out. Melissa's mind was fucked. Though hesitant, Melissa allowed love in. Melissa regained something eternal.

God is sick. God is mentally ill. God is not patient. God is not kind. God is envious. God is boastful. God is arrogant. God is rude. God insists on God's own way. God is irritable. God is resentful. God forgets the truth. God bears nothing. God believes nothing. God has no hope. God has no endurance. God is sick. God is mentally ill.

God is love. God is mentally ill. God is patient. God is kind. God is not envious. God is not boastful. God is not arrogant. God is not rude. God doesn't insist on God's own way. God is not irritable. God is not resentful. God is the truth. God bears all things. God believes all things. God hopes all things. God endures all things. God is love. God is mentally ill.

Psychotic realities are complicated. God is mentally ill. In the midst of the chaos of the divine mind, God is complex. Like all persons who are mentally ill, God embodies both sickness and love. Which one is God? To describe God as one thing or the other is to describe something other than God. In the end, God is both.

Since Keith was a young child, everyone knew that he was mentally ill. Sometimes, Keith was very loving. Sometimes, Keith would explode with rage. Voices in Keith's head seemed to occasionally control his actions. One day, Keith violently attacked someone for no reason. While in prison, Keith wrestled with his head. In court, one of Keith's friends testified that Keith was one of the most loving people that he'd ever met and also one of the most violent people that he'd ever met. The judge snapped back, "Which Keith is the real Keith?" Keith's friend didn't hesitate, "They both are."

Revelation

"The one who testifies to these things says, 'Surely I am coming soon.'"—Revelation 22:20

War erupted in the mind of God. Darkness collided into light. Violence raged. Despite the strength of the darkness, light refused to be defeated and kept fighting back. In anguished anticipation, God rolled back and forth. God felt like God was a part of the battle. Light threw the darkness out of the mind of God. For a moment, God felt tremendous relief. Then, the darkness came back stronger. God knew that the darkness would rage against the mind of God forever. Regardless, God was more prepared than ever to fight back.

Everyone knew that a war was going on in Willie's mind. Rocking back and forth, Willie looked like she was a million miles away. The darkness wrestled with the light in Willie's mind. Violence raged in Willie's eyes. Words of terror filled Willie's ears. Willie rolled between darkness and light. Willie kept fighting. Willie knew that she was in a battle for her mind. Eventually, light threw the darkness. Relief flooded Willie's entire being. There was peace for a moment. However, the darkness didn't quit. Ultimately, the darkness came back stronger than ever. Willie didn't give a shit. For the first time, Willie knew that she could beat the darkness.

God kept seeing the beasts. There was the beast named depression. There was the beast named mania. There was the beast named psychosis. God was ready for them. God pushed depression back with light. Though God couldn't kill the beast, God knew that God wouldn't be destroyed by it. God tossed mania back with control. God wasn't able to kill the beast. God was only able to manage it. God kicked psychosis back with clearness. God fought until psychosis was subdued. Though God never stops wrestling with the beasts, God is winning. The beasts will not control God. God will control the beasts.

Mugabe knew the beasts by name. There was anxiety. There was psychosis. There was depression. The beasts troubled Mugabe day and night. Finally, Mugabe got the tools to fight back. One by one, Mugabe learned to manage the beasts. Ultimately, Mugabe found a way to start winning. Now, Mugabe controls the beasts. The beasts don't control Mugabe.

Treatment was the river of life God so desperately needed. There was no future before God got treatment. Now, there was a little light. The little light poked holes in the darkness of God's mind and granted God the ability to be a light for others. Slowly, God is coming to collect all who suffer from mental illness. Heaven is God's treatment center. There, God will join the mentally ill from all of time and space to be treated and reach for a future together. God knows that mental illness can't be cured. Treatment is eternal.

Laurie was mentally ill. On multiple occasions, Laurie crashed and ended up in various mental health facilities. After her last treatment, Laurie wanted to help others. Securing a job at the local mental health clinic, Laurie was in charge of speaking with those who were in need of help. Laurie was a gatherer. Day after day, Laurie joined all of those who were suffering and helped them reach for a future. Laurie knew that her place was amongst the mentally ill. Laurie knows mental illness can't be cured. Treatment is eternal.

End
"Amen."—Revelation 22:21

God is here with us. We are mentally ill. God is mentally ill. God suffers with us. The entire scripture is the story of a mentally ill people interacting with a mentally ill God. The mentally ill God does not die at the end of scripture. On the contrary, God still struggles through eternity with a psychosis that God will never shake. God is here with us. God joins us in our mental illness. We are the fucked up brain of God. We are the end of any doubt that mental illness comes from anywhere but God. We are the great "Amen." We are the psychosis of God.

Conclusion

"I AM WHO I AM."—Exodus 3:14

IN THE BEGINNING, GOD dwelled in our stories. In the story, God dwelled in our stories. In the now, God dwells in our stories. For eternity, God will dwell in our stories. God lives in story. Theology is about using the image of God to connect with God. There is no God without the image of God. Connection to God comes through stories . . . our stories. The embodiment of God in our stories is what makes God . . . God. Our stories are always moving and changing. Our stories are always growing and developing. Our stories never end. There is always more to our stories. God is always out there moving and changing. God is always out there growing and developing. The story of God never ends. There is always more to the God story. We can only capture a glimpse of the God story through piecing together pieces of our stories. The Psychosis of God is The Psychosis of Us. We are mentally ill. We are the very image of God. Liberation comes through finding God within and without. Our stories are the story of God. We must have the courage to place God in our context. We must have the courage to believe in the mentally ill God. The psychosis of God is what makes God believable. The psychosis of God is what makes God holy. The psychosis of God is what makes true. We must have the courage to believe in crazy.

"A tornado just came right through here!" Traffic signals littered the ground. Cars were pushed off the road. Buildings were blown apart. Destruction was everywhere. I looked at my hands. I couldn't stop shaking. Fear swept through my young body. I couldn't catch my heart. "We need to get home. There could be another one at any moment." I hung on to those last few words. For about six months, I was prepared for a tornado to hit at any moment. I couldn't eat. I couldn't sleep. I never felt safe. Anxiety was all that I knew. The attacks were unlike anything I ever felt. Wind would unleash terror in brain. My teachers at school would force me to go outside. I stayed right next to the door. I just knew the tornado was going to hit. No one helped me. Incessantly, I prayed for God to save me from the potential tornado. Depression and mania cycled in my brain. Both were terrifying. Both were dangerous. I didn't grow out of it. I just moved on to another fixation. "God be with me."

"The end of the world could come tonight." Repeatedly, I went to the front of the room and got saved. I didn't want to get left behind. I wanted to go to heaven. I prayed over and over. Every night, I went home terrified that tonight was going to be the night that I was going to finally get left behind. Anxiety attacks hit me late at night. I would shake in fear. I had trouble controlling my body. I just knew that I wasn't really saved. Our youth leaders told us that we had to know that we know that we know that we know. I never felt like I fully knew. Knowledge always seemed fleeting in those hyperevangelistic settings. For three years, I cycled through mania around praying to get saved and depression about feeling like I wasn't saved. Each time I tried to talk to someone, I was told that I needed to pray about it. I prayed for three years straight. Fear was a constant presence. Nothing worked. I just was manipulated. "God save me."

"How can God send billions of people to hell?" The question haunted me. I struggled with whether or not I still believed what I was preaching. More questions flooded my mind. The questions never stopped. I felt like I was being beat with questions. I felt like the questions only lead to deeper and deeper depressions. What was I supposed to do? I was training to be a minister and I couldn't get past the questions. Suicide seemed like a good option. There would be no more questions after I took my last breath. No one could figure out what was wrong with me. I couldn't function.

I couldn't eat. I couldn't sleep. I was miserable. I felt so alone. "Where are you God?"

The cycles come often. God is always in them. The mania cripples the body. The depression cripples the mind. The numbness cripples the soul. Though the elements of psychosis are different for everyone who suffers from mental illness, there is always suffering. One cannot be who they are. One cannot be saved. One cannot engage the questions. One can't be. One can't save. One can't question. God understands. God has the same struggles that we do. God struggles to figure out who God is. God is desperate to be saved from God. God finds questions of God terrifying. God struggles in being. God struggles in saving. God struggles in questioning. God knows the states. Confusion is confusing. Anxiety is anxious. Crazy is crazy. Depression is depressed. Mania is manic. Psychosis is psychotic. The list could go on and on. God knows every possible state of mental health . . . God lives them eternally. The mentally ill are the reflection of God. God is in the mentally ill. God is mentally ill.

We must never forget God's story. God broke down. God needed treatment. God needed medication. God didn't respond well. God had to be institutionalized. God had to recover. God had to exist. God is still seeking to be in the midst of mental illness. We are with God in the midst of God's struggles. God is with us in the midst our struggles. Our story is only found in the psychosis of God.

I don't trust people with normal minds. Normal minds produce normal things. Normal things are always opposed to the things of a queer God. Is there anything normal about being the God beyond conception? Is there anything normal about God's creation of humanity in God's image? Is there anything normal about God choosing to become human? Is there anything normal about God? God is not normal. God's mind is not normal. God's mind is queer. Why does everyone chase normal minds? God will never be found in normal. The queer minds of the mentally ill are closest to God because they carry the mind of God. In a world of normal minds, the queer minds of the mentally ill are the path to

God. I don't trust people with normal minds. I trust those whose minds emulate our God. I trust the mentally ill.

In Matthew 25:40, God assures us that God is most present in the "least of these" amongst us. Throughout time and space, the mentally ill have been the least of these. God is in the mentally ill. The mentally ill are our path to God. Listen to the psychosis. Feel the psychosis. Know psychosis. Listen to God. Feel God. Know God. The mentally ill are God amongst us. We can't find God without going crazy.

The chaos of psychosis has much to teach us. God is learning to exist in the darkness. The mentally ill are learning to be the light. God is learning to exist in the midst of confusion. The mentally ill are learning to be confused. God is learning to hold on. The mentally ill are learning to be. The psychosis never stops. The chaos never stops. The learning never stops. We don't know where we're going. We only know where we are found. We are found in the psychosis of the God.

Benediction

Go. Embrace the mystery of the mind. Embrace the mystery of God. Live in the chaos and transform the cosmos.

Amen.

Scripture Index

OLD TESTAMENT

NEW TESTAMENT

www.ingramcontent.com/pod-product-compliance
Lightning Source LLC
Chambersburg PA
CBHW071103090426
42737CB00013B/2456